Cybersecurity Handbook for Beginners

By

Mark David

Table of contents

Introduction

Why Cybersecurity Matters

In today's interconnected world, the importance of cybersecurity cannot be overstated. The digital landscape has become an integral part of our lives, encompassing everything from social interactions and financial transactions to essential services and national infrastructure. With the increasing reliance on digital technologies, the need to protect these systems and the data they handle has never been more critical.

Cybersecurity is essential for several reasons. First, it safeguards our personal information. Whether it's our banking details, medical records, or social media activities, the information we store and share online is valuable not only to us but also to malicious actors. Protecting this information is vital to prevent identity theft, financial loss, and other forms of personal harm.

Second, cybersecurity is crucial for businesses of all sizes. A successful cyber attack can cripple a business, leading to financial losses, damage to reputation, and in some cases, closure. Small businesses are particularly vulnerable, as they often lack the resources to recover from a significant breach. For larger organizations, cybersecurity is not just a matter of protecting assets but also of maintaining customer trust and compliance with regulatory requirements.

On a broader scale, cybersecurity is vital for national security. Cyber attacks can target critical infrastructure such as power grids, transportation systems, and communication networks, potentially causing widespread disruption and harm. Additionally, state-sponsored cyber espionage and cyber warfare are growing threats that can have far-reaching geopolitical consequences.

In essence, cybersecurity matters because it is the first line of defense in a world where the stakes are incredibly high. Protecting our digital lives is not just about avoiding inconvenience—it's about safeguarding our identities, our businesses, and even our society's stability.

Common Cyber Threats

The digital world is rife with threats, ranging from simple scams to sophisticated attacks carried out by organized criminal groups or state-sponsored entities. Understanding these threats is the first step in defending against them. Here's an overview of some of the most common cyber threats:

1. **Phishing:** Phishing attacks are one of the most prevalent forms of cybercrime. They involve tricking individuals into divulging sensitive information, such as passwords or credit card numbers, by pretending to be a trustworthy entity. This is often done through fake emails, websites, or text messages that appear legitimate but are designed to steal your information.

2. **Malware:** Malware, short for malicious software, is a broad category that includes viruses, worms, trojans, and spyware. Once installed on a device, malware can perform a variety of harmful actions, from stealing sensitive data to hijacking the device for use in other attacks. Malware often spreads through infected email attachments, software downloads, or compromised websites.

3. **Ransomware:** Ransomware is a specific type of malware that encrypts a victim's files and demands payment (often in

cryptocurrency) in exchange for the decryption key. Ransomware attacks can be devastating for individuals and organizations alike, as they can result in the loss of critical data and significant financial costs.

4. **Social Engineering:** Social engineering attacks exploit human psychology to trick victims into revealing confidential information or performing actions that compromise security. Phishing is a type of social engineering, but other methods include pretexting, baiting, and tailgating, all of which rely on manipulation rather than technical hacking skills.

5. **Man-in-the-Middle (MitM) Attacks:** In a MitM attack, the attacker intercepts and alters communication between two parties without their knowledge. This can occur, for example, when a user connects to an unsecured public Wi-Fi network, allowing the attacker to eavesdrop on their

activities or even inject malicious content into the communication.

6. Denial of Service (DoS) Attacks: DoS attacks aim to overwhelm a system, network, or website with traffic, rendering it unavailable to users. Distributed Denial of Service (DDoS) attacks amplify this by using multiple compromised devices (often part of a botnet) to flood the target with requests. These attacks can cause significant disruption to services and are often used as a distraction while other attacks are carried out.

7. Advanced Persistent Threats (APTs): APTs are long-term, targeted attacks carried out by highly skilled and well-funded adversaries, often with a specific objective, such as espionage or data theft. APTs typically infiltrate a network undetected, remaining in place for extended periods to gather information or achieve their goal.

8. **Zero-Day Exploits:** Zero-day exploits take advantage of previously unknown vulnerabilities in software or hardware. Since the vendor is unaware of the flaw, there is no immediate fix available, making zero-day attacks particularly dangerous.

These threats represent just a portion of the vast and evolving cybersecurity landscape. As technology advances, so do the methods used by cybercriminals, making it essential for everyone—from individuals to large organizations—to stay informed and vigilant.

The Goal of This Handbook

The field of cybersecurity can be intimidating, especially for beginners. The terminology, the technical aspects, and the sheer volume of information can be overwhelming. The goal of this handbook is to demystify cybersecurity, making it accessible and understandable for everyone, regardless of their technical background.

By the end of this handbook, readers will have a solid foundation in cybersecurity principles. They will understand the most common threats and how to protect themselves against them. The handbook will provide practical, actionable advice on securing personal devices, safeguarding online accounts, and responding effectively to potential cyber incidents.

This handbook is designed to empower readers with the knowledge and tools they need to take control of their digital security. It is not just about learning what the threats are but also about understanding how to develop habits and practices that will keep them safe in the digital world. Whether you're a complete novice or someone looking to refresh your knowledge, this handbook will serve as a comprehensive guide to building a strong cybersecurity foundation.

Through clear explanations, real-world examples, and step-by-step instructions, readers will gain the confidence to navigate the digital world securely. Ultimately, the goal is to make cybersecurity a part of your everyday life—simple, manageable, and effective.

Chapter 1:

Understanding the Basics

What is Cybersecurity?

Cybersecurity refers to the practice of protecting systems, networks, and data from digital attacks, theft, and damage. It encompasses a wide range of technologies, processes, and practices designed to defend computers, servers, mobile devices, electronic systems, networks, and data from malicious intrusions. In simpler terms, cybersecurity is about keeping your digital information and devices safe from unauthorized access and harm.

At its core, cybersecurity aims to ensure three key principles:

1. **Confidentiality**: Ensuring that sensitive information is accessed only by authorized individuals.

2. **Integrity**: Protecting information from being altered by unauthorized parties.

3. **Availability**: Ensuring that authorized users have reliable access to information and resources when needed.

These principles, often abbreviated as CIA, form the foundation of cybersecurity and guide the development of security measures and protocols. Cybersecurity is not just about protecting against external threats; it also involves safeguarding against insider threats, whether intentional or accidental.

In the modern world, cybersecurity extends beyond just computers and servers. It covers everything connected to the internet—smartphones, tablets, IoT devices, and even critical infrastructure like power grids and water supply systems. As our reliance on technology grows, so does the importance of cybersecurity in safeguarding our digital lives.

Key Terminologies

Understanding some key terminologies is essential for grasping the basics of cybersecurity. Below are definitions of some fundamental terms:

1. **Firewall**:
   A firewall is a network security device that monitors and controls incoming and outgoing network traffic based on predetermined security rules. It acts as a barrier between a trusted internal network and untrusted external networks, such as the internet. Firewalls can be hardware-based, software-based, or a combination of both. Their primary function is to block unauthorized access while allowing legitimate communication to pass through.

2. **Encryption**:

Encryption is the process of converting data into a coded format that can only be read by someone who has the correct decryption key. This ensures that even if data is intercepted by an unauthorized party, it remains unreadable and secure. Encryption is widely used to protect sensitive information, such as credit card numbers, passwords, and personal communications.

3. **Malware**:

Malware, short for malicious software, refers to any software designed to cause harm to a computer, network, or user. Malware includes viruses, worms, trojans, ransomware, spyware, and adware. Each type of malware has its own method of spreading and causing damage, but they all aim to disrupt normal operations, steal data, or exploit vulnerabilities.

4. **Phishing**:

Phishing is a type of social engineering attack where an attacker disguises themselves as a trustworthy entity to trick individuals into divulging sensitive information, such as login credentials or financial details. Phishing attacks are typically carried out through email, fake websites, or text messages that appear legitimate but are actually fraudulent.

5. **Antivirus**:

Antivirus software is a program designed to detect, prevent, and remove malware from computers and networks. It works by scanning files and programs for known malware signatures and suspicious behavior. While antivirus software is an essential component of cybersecurity, it is not foolproof and should be used in conjunction with other security measures.

6. **Two-Factor Authentication (2FA):**

Two-factor authentication is a security process that requires users to provide two different forms of identification to access an account or system. Typically, 2FA combines something you know (like a password) with something you have (like a smartphone or hardware token) or something you are (like a fingerprint). This added layer of security makes it more difficult for attackers to gain unauthorized access.

7. VPN (Virtual Private Network):

A VPN is a service that creates a secure, encrypted connection between your device and the internet. This connection helps protect your online activity from eavesdropping, censorship, and tracking. VPNs are commonly used to access region-restricted content, protect data on public Wi-Fi networks, and maintain privacy.

8. Zero-Day Exploit:

A zero-day exploit is a cyber attack that targets a previously unknown vulnerability in software or hardware. Since the vulnerability is unknown to the vendor, there is no patch or fix available, making zero-day exploits particularly dangerous. Attackers can use these exploits to gain unauthorized access, steal data, or cause other harm before the vulnerability is discovered and patched.

9. **Social Engineering:**

Social engineering is the manipulation of individuals into performing actions or divulging confidential information. Rather than exploiting technical vulnerabilities, social engineering attacks rely on human psychology to deceive victims. Common techniques include phishing, pretexting, baiting, and tailgating.

10. **Botnet:**

A botnet is a network of compromised computers or devices (often called "bots" or "zombies") that are controlled remotely by an attacker, usually without the knowledge of the device owners. Botnets are often used to carry out large-scale attacks, such as Distributed Denial of Service (DDoS) attacks, where the bots flood a target system with traffic, overwhelming it and causing it to crash.

Understanding these terms will help you navigate the world of cybersecurity and better comprehend the threats and defenses involved.

How Cyber Attacks Happen

Cyber attacks can occur in a variety of ways, and understanding the basic methods used by hackers is crucial for defending against them. Below are some common tactics employed by cybercriminals:

1. **Phishing Attacks:**

Phishing is one of the most common methods used by hackers to steal sensitive information. Attackers send fraudulent emails or messages that appear to be from legitimate sources, such as banks, social media platforms, or online services. These messages often contain links to fake websites designed to capture login credentials, credit card numbers, or other personal information. In some cases, phishing emails may also include malicious attachments that can install malware on the victim's device.

2. Malware Infections:

Hackers use various types of malware to infect devices and networks. This can occur through email attachments, malicious websites, or software downloads. Once installed, malware can perform a wide range of harmful activities, such as stealing data, spying on users, or taking control of the device. Ransomware, a particularly dangerous type of malware, encrypts the victim's files and demands payment for their release.

3. Exploiting Vulnerabilities:

Cybercriminals often look for vulnerabilities in software, hardware, or network configurations that they can exploit. These vulnerabilities may be the result of unpatched software, misconfigured systems, or weak passwords. Once a vulnerability is discovered, hackers can use it to gain unauthorized access, escalate privileges, or execute malicious code. Zero-day exploits are particularly dangerous because they target vulnerabilities that are unknown to the software vendor, leaving systems exposed until a patch is developed.

4. Social Engineering:

Social engineering attacks rely on manipulating individuals rather than exploiting technical flaws. Hackers may impersonate someone trustworthy to deceive victims into revealing confidential information or performing actions that compromise security. For example, an attacker might pose as an IT support technician and ask a victim to provide their login credentials or disable security settings. Social engineering is often used in conjunction with other attack methods to increase the chances of success.

5. Denial of Service (DoS) Attacks:

DoS attacks aim to disrupt the availability of a service or network by overwhelming it with traffic. In a basic DoS attack, the hacker floods a target system with requests, causing it to slow down or crash. A more sophisticated version, known as a Distributed Denial of Service (DDoS) attack, involves multiple compromised devices (often part of a botnet) simultaneously targeting the same system. These attacks can cause significant disruption, especially for online services and websites.

6. Man-in-the-Middle (MitM) Attacks:

In a MitM attack, the hacker intercepts and potentially alters communication between two parties without their knowledge. This can occur when users connect to unsecured public Wi-Fi networks or when an attacker compromises a network's security. The hacker can eavesdrop on the communication, steal sensitive information, or inject malicious content. For example, an attacker might intercept login credentials as they are transmitted over an unsecured connection.

7. **Brute Force Attacks:**

In a brute force attack, the hacker attempts to guess a password or encryption key by systematically trying all possible combinations. While this method can be time-consuming, it can be effective against weak passwords or poorly implemented encryption. Hackers often use automated tools to speed up the process, trying thousands or even millions of combinations in a short period. Once the correct password is found, the hacker gains unauthorized access to the account or system.

8. SQL Injection:

SQL injection is a technique used by hackers to exploit vulnerabilities in web applications that interact with databases. By inserting malicious SQL code into input fields, the attacker can manipulate the database to reveal sensitive information, such as user data, or even take control of the database itself. SQL injection attacks are possible when user inputs are not properly validated or sanitized by the application.

9. Credential Stuffing:

Credential stuffing involves using stolen login credentials, often obtained from data breaches, to gain unauthorized access to multiple accounts. Since many people reuse passwords across different services, hackers can use automated tools to test stolen credentials on a wide range of websites. If the credentials are valid on any of these sites, the hacker gains access to the account.

10. **Insider Threats:**

Not all cyber attacks come from external sources. Insider threats involve employees, contractors, or other trusted individuals who intentionally or accidentally cause harm to an organization's cybersecurity. This can include actions such as leaking confidential information, installing malware, or bypassing security controls. Insider threats can be particularly challenging to detect and prevent because they involve individuals with legitimate access to the organization's systems.

Understanding how cyber attacks happen is the first step in defending

Chapter 2:

Securing Your Devices

In today's digital age, our devices are constantly connected to the internet, making them potential targets for cyber threats. Securing your devices is the first line of defense in protecting your personal information, maintaining your privacy, and ensuring the integrity of your data. This chapter will explore essential security measures for personal computers, mobile devices, and Internet of Things (IoT) devices, providing practical advice on how to safeguard these critical components of your digital life.

Protecting Personal Computers

Personal computers (PCs) are central to our digital activities, from managing finances and storing personal information to communicating and working remotely. Given their importance, securing your PC is crucial. Below are some fundamental security measures every PC owner should implement:

1. **Keep Your Operating System and Software Updated:**
   - Why It Matters: Operating system (OS) and software updates often include patches for security vulnerabilities that hackers can exploit. Failing to update your OS and software leaves your computer exposed to these vulnerabilities.
   - **How to Implement**: Enable automatic updates for your OS and key software applications. Regularly check for updates manually if automatic updates are not available. For example, Windows and macOS both have built-in update tools that can be set to download and install updates automatically.

2. Install and Maintain Antivirus Software:

- **Why It Matters:** Antivirus software is designed to detect, prevent, and remove malware from your computer. While it's not a foolproof solution, it provides a critical layer of defense against known threats.

- **How to Implement:** Choose a reputable antivirus program and keep it updated to ensure it can detect the latest threats. Run regular scans of your system and set the software to scan incoming files and emails in real time. Many antivirus programs also offer additional features like firewalls, email protection, and safe browsing tools.

3. Use a Firewall:

- **Why It Matters:** A firewall acts as a barrier between your computer and the internet, controlling incoming and outgoing traffic based on predetermined security rules. It helps block unauthorized access to your system.

- How to Implement: Most operating systems come with a built-in firewall (e.g., Windows Defender Firewall). Ensure it is enabled and configured correctly. If you prefer additional features, consider using a third-party firewall solution. Firewalls can be set to block specific applications, monitor network traffic, and provide alerts when suspicious activity is detected.

4. Enable Full-Disk Encryption:

- Why It Matters: Full-disk encryption protects the data on your hard drive by converting it into a format that cannot be read without the correct decryption key or password. This is especially important if your computer is lost or stolen.

- How to Implement: On Windows, BitLocker is a built-in encryption tool, while macOS users can use FileVault. Both tools can encrypt your entire hard drive, ensuring that your data remains secure even if someone gains physical access to your computer.

5. Practice Safe Browsing:

- **Why It Matters:** The web is a common vector for malware and phishing attacks. Practicing safe browsing habits reduces the risk of encountering malicious websites or inadvertently downloading harmful content.

- **How to Implement:** Avoid clicking on suspicious links or downloading files from untrusted sources. Use a secure, privacy-focused browser (like Mozilla Firefox or Google Chrome with privacy extensions) and enable features such as pop-up blockers and safe browsing tools. Consider using browser extensions like HTTPS Everywhere to ensure your connection is encrypted and Privacy Badger to block tracking scripts.

6. Use Strong, Unique Passwords:

- **Why It Matters:** Weak or reused passwords are a common entry point for hackers. A strong, unique password for each of your accounts and devices is essential for maintaining security.

 - **How to Implement:** Create passwords that are at least 12 characters long, combining letters, numbers, and symbols. Use a password manager to generate and store unique passwords for each account, reducing the risk of password reuse. Many password managers also offer features like secure notes and two-factor authentication (2FA) integration.

7. **Enable Two-Factor Authentication (2FA):**

 - **Why It Matters:** 2FA adds an additional layer of security by requiring a second form of verification in addition to your password. This could be a code sent to your phone, a biometric factor like a fingerprint, or a hardware token.

 - **How to Implement:** Whenever possible, enable 2FA on your accounts and devices. For your PC, this might involve using a combination of a password and a fingerprint or a security key. Most major services and devices offer 2FA as an option in their security settings.

8. **Regularly Back Up Your Data:**
   - **Why It Matters:** Backing up your data ensures that you can recover your important files in case of a cyber attack, hardware failure, or other data loss events.
   - **How to Implement:** Use a combination of local and cloud-based backup solutions. Windows offers a built-in backup feature, and macOS has Time Machine. Additionally, consider using cloud services like Google Drive, Dropbox, or OneDrive for real-time file synchronization and backup.

9. **Be Cautious with External Devices:**
   - **Why It Matters:** External devices like USB drives and external hard drives can carry malware and other threats. When you connect these devices to your computer, you risk infecting your system.

- **How to Implement:** Scan external devices with antivirus software before accessing their contents. Avoid using untrusted or unfamiliar USB drives, and disable the "AutoRun" feature on your PC to prevent automatic execution of potentially harmful files.

By implementing these basic security measures, you can significantly reduce the risk of cyber attacks on your personal computer and safeguard your digital life.

Mobile Device Security

Smartphones and tablets have become indispensable tools for communication, work, and entertainment. However, their portability and constant connectivity also make them attractive targets for cybercriminals. Securing your mobile devices is essential to protect your personal information and maintain your privacy.

Here are best practices for securing your smartphones and tablets:

1. **Keep Your Device Updated:**

- **Why It Matters:** Like computers, mobile devices receive regular updates that include security patches to fix vulnerabilities. Keeping your device updated helps protect it from the latest threats.

- **How to Implement:** Enable automatic updates for your operating system and apps. Regularly check for updates manually, especially if your device is set to update only over Wi-Fi or when plugged in. Both Android and iOS provide settings to automate updates.

2. **Use Strong Authentication:**

- **Why It Matters:** Strong authentication methods, such as biometrics (fingerprint or facial recognition) or a robust passcode, add an essential layer of security to your mobile device, making it harder for unauthorized users to access your data.

- **How to Implement:** Set up a passcode or password that is difficult to guess, and enable biometric authentication if your device supports it. Avoid using simple patterns or PINs, as these can be easily guessed or observed. On iOS, you can set a six-digit PIN or an alphanumeric password, while Android offers similar options, along with fingerprint and facial recognition features.

3. Install Security Apps:
- **Why It Matters:** Security apps can help protect your device from malware, phishing attempts, and other threats. They often include features like anti-theft tools, safe browsing, and device scanning.

- **How to Implement:** Choose a reputable mobile security app, such as Avast Mobile Security, Norton Mobile Security, or McAfee Mobile Security, and install it on your device. These apps can scan for malware, block suspicious websites, and provide anti-theft features like remote lock and wipe.

4. Limit App Permissions:

- **Why It Matters:** Apps often request access to various functions and data on your device, such as your location, contacts, and camera. Granting unnecessary permissions can expose you to privacy risks.

- **How to Implement:** Review the permissions requested by each app during installation and only grant those that are necessary for the app's functionality. Regularly check and adjust app permissions in your device's settings. Both Android and iOS allow you to manage permissions for individual apps, such as location, camera, microphone, and contacts.

5. Enable Remote Wipe:

- **Why It Matters:** If your device is lost or stolen, remote wipe allows you to erase all data on the device, preventing unauthorized access to your information.

- **How to Implement:** Set up remote wipe through services like Find My iPhone (iOS) or Find My Device (Android). These tools also allow you to locate your device, lock it remotely, and display a message to someone who may find it.

6. Avoid Public Wi-Fi for Sensitive Transactions:

- **Why It Matters:** Public Wi-Fi networks are often unsecured, making it easier for hackers to intercept your data. Using public Wi-Fi for sensitive activities like banking or shopping can expose you to risks.

- **How to Implement:** Use a VPN (Virtual Private Network) when connecting to public Wi-Fi to encrypt your data and protect your privacy. Alternatively, use your mobile data connection for sensitive transactions. Many mobile security apps also offer built-in VPN services.

7. Be Cautious with App Downloads:

- **Why It Matters:** Downloading apps from unofficial or untrusted sources increases the risk of installing malware or spyware on your device.

- **How to Implement:** Only download apps from official app stores like Google Play (Android) or the App Store (iOS). Even in official stores, be cautious—check app reviews, permissions, and developer information before downloading. Avoid sideloading apps (installing apps from sources other than the official store) unless you are confident in the app's safety.

8. Enable Encryption:

- **Matters**: Encryption on your mobile device ensures that your data is secure even if someone gains physical access to it. When your device is encrypted, all data stored on it is scrambled and can only be accessed by someone with the correct decryption key, which is typically tied to your passcode or biometric authentication.

- **How to Implement**: Most modern smartphones come with encryption enabled by default. On Android devices, you can check and enable encryption in the security settings. For iPhones, data encryption is automatically enabled when you set a passcode. Always ensure your device is encrypted, especially if you store sensitive information on it.

9. **Regularly Back Up Your Mobile Device:**
- **Why It Matters**: Regular backups ensure that you can recover your data in case of a loss, such as from a cyber attack, theft, or hardware failure. Backups allow you to restore your device to a previous state without losing important information.
- **How to Implement**: Use cloud services like iCloud (for iOS) or Google Drive (for Android) to automatically back up your data. Additionally, you can perform manual backups to your computer using iTunes (for iOS) or USB cable transfers (for Android).

Set up regular backup intervals to ensure your data is always protected.

10. **Be Aware of Phishing and Social Engineering Attacks:**

- **Why It Matters**: Phishing and social engineering attacks are common on mobile devices, often coming through emails, text messages, or apps. Falling victim to these attacks can lead to the compromise of your personal data or even the loss of access to your device.

- **How to Implement**: Be skeptical of unexpected messages, especially those asking for personal information or urging immediate action. Avoid clicking on links or downloading attachments from unknown or untrusted sources. If you receive a suspicious message, verify its legitimacy through official channels before taking any action.

11. **Disable Bluetooth and NFC When Not in Use:**

- **Why It Matters**: Bluetooth and Near Field Communication (NFC) are useful features, but they can also be exploited by attackers to access your device without your knowledge. Disabling these features when not in use reduces your exposure to such threats.

- **How to Implement**: Turn off Bluetooth and NFC in your device's settings when you're not actively using them. This practice not only improves security but also conserves battery life. If you need to use these features, make sure to pair only with trusted devices and avoid accepting unexpected connection requests.

By following these best practices, you can significantly enhance the security of your mobile devices, protecting both your personal data and your privacy.

IoT Devices

The Internet of Things (IoT) refers to the network of smart devices connected to the internet, ranging from smart thermostats and home security cameras to wearable fitness trackers and smart appliances. While these devices offer convenience and automation, they also introduce new security risks, as many IoT devices lack robust security features. Securing your IoT devices is crucial to protect your home network and personal information.

1. **Change Default Passwords:**

- **Why It Matters**: Many IoT devices come with default usernames and passwords that are widely known and easily accessible to hackers. Failing to change these default credentials makes your devices vulnerable to unauthorized access.

- How to Implement: Upon setting up a new IoT device, immediately change the default password to a strong, unique password. Avoid using simple or easily guessable passwords. If your device allows, enable two-factor authentication for an added layer of security.

2. Regularly Update Firmware:

- Why It Matters: IoT devices, like any other technology, may have vulnerabilities that manufacturers address through firmware updates. Keeping your devices' firmware up-to-date is essential to protect them from known security flaws.

- How to Implement: Check for firmware updates regularly through the device's app or website. Some devices allow you to enable automatic updates, which is recommended if available. Regular updates ensure that your devices are equipped with the latest security patches.

3. Segment Your Home Network:

- **Why It Matters:** Connecting all your devices to a single network can expose your entire system if one device is compromised. Segmenting your home network into separate zones for IoT devices and other critical devices (like computers and smartphones) can limit the potential damage of a security breach.

- **How to Implement:** Set up a guest network on your router specifically for your IoT devices. This network should be isolated from your main network, which is used for more critical devices. Most modern routers offer the option to create multiple networks with different security settings.

4. Disable Unnecessary Features:

- **Why It Matters**: Many IoT devices come with features that are not essential for their operation but can introduce security risks, such as remote access, Universal Plug and Play (UPnP), and voice activation. Disabling unnecessary features reduces the attack surface of your devices.

- **How to Implement:** Review the settings on each of your IoT devices and disable any features that you do not use or need. For instance, if you do not need remote access to a device, turn it off in the settings. Similarly, disable UPnP on your router unless you have a specific need for it, as it can expose your network to outside threats.

5. **Monitor Device Activity:**
- **Why It Matters:** Monitoring the activity of your IoT devices can help you detect unusual behavior that may indicate a security breach. Many IoT devices communicate with external servers, and unexpected or excessive data traffic can be a sign of compromise.

- **How to Implement:** Use network monitoring tools, such as those provided by your router or third-party apps, to keep an eye on the traffic generated by your IoT devices. Look for spikes in activity, connections to unfamiliar servers, or other suspicious behavior. If you notice anything unusual, investigate further and take appropriate action, such as disconnecting the device or resetting it to factory settings.

6. **Secure Your Wi-Fi Network:**

- **Why It Matters:** Your Wi-Fi network is the gateway to all your connected devices. An unsecured network can allow unauthorized users to access your IoT devices and potentially control them or intercept your data.

- **How to Implement:** Ensure your Wi-Fi network is secured with a strong password and WPA3 encryption (or WPA2 if WPA3 is not available). Avoid using WEP, as it is outdated and easily compromised. Additionally, consider disabling Wi-Fi Protected Setup (WPS), which can be exploited by attackers.

7. **Be Aware of the Data Your Devices Collect:**

- **Why It Matters:** Many IoT devices collect data about your habits, environment, and even personal information. Understanding what data is being collected and how it is used is crucial for maintaining your privacy.

- **How to Implement:** Review the privacy policies of your IoT devices and services to understand what data they collect and how it is stored, used, and shared. Where possible, opt out of data collection or choose devices and services that prioritize user privacy. Some devices may offer settings to limit data collection or anonymize it.

8. Physically Secure Your Devices:

- **Why It Matters:** Physical access to an IoT device can allow an attacker to tamper with it, reset it, or gain control over it. Securing the physical location of your devices adds an additional layer of security.

- **How to Implement:** Place IoT devices in secure, hard-to-reach locations where they are not easily accessible to unauthorized individuals. For outdoor devices, such as security cameras, consider using tamper-resistant mounts and enclosures. Additionally, ensure that any devices with physical reset buttons are secured to prevent unauthorized use.

9. **Use Trusted Brands and Devices:**
- **Why It Matters:** Not all IoT devices are created equal. Some manufacturers prioritize security, while others may cut corners to reduce costs, leading to insecure devices. Choosing reputable brands and devices can reduce the risk of security vulnerabilities.

- **How to Implement:** Research and choose IoT devices from manufacturers with a strong reputation for security and privacy. Look for devices that receive regular firmware updates and support from the manufacturer. Reading reviews and checking for third-party security certifications can also help in making informed decisions.

10. Regularly Review and Audit Your Devices:

- **Why It Matters:** Over time, you may accumulate several IoT devices that you no longer use or need. These devices can become security liabilities if left connected to your network.

- **How to Implement:** Periodically review all IoT devices connected to your network. Identify any devices that are no longer in use and disconnect them. Perform regular audits of your device settings, firmware, and security configurations to ensure everything is up to date and secure.

Securing IoT devices is an ongoing process that requires awareness and proactive measures. By following these best practices, you can help ensure that your smart home remains safe from cyber threats and that your personal information is protected.

Chapter 3:

Safe Internet Practices

The internet has become an integral part of daily life, connecting us to an infinite amount of information, people, and services. However, with these conveniences come significant risks. Cybercriminals constantly look for opportunities to exploit unsuspecting users, making it critical to adopt safe internet practices. This chapter will guide you through three key areas: recognizing phishing scams, creating strong passwords, and using public Wi-Fi safely.

Recognizing Phishing Scams

Phishing scams are one of the most prevalent and dangerous types of cyber threats. These scams typically involve fraudulent communications, such as emails, text messages, or websites, designed to trick recipients into divulging personal information like usernames, passwords, or credit card details.

Understanding Phishing

Phishing is a form of social engineering—a tactic used by attackers to manipulate individuals into revealing confidential information. Cybercriminals often impersonate trusted entities, such as banks, social media platforms, or even colleagues, to make their attacks appear legitimate. The ultimate goal of phishing is to gain unauthorized access to sensitive data, which can then be used for identity theft, financial fraud, or further cyber attacks.

Types of Phishing Scams
1. **Email Phishing:**
   - **Description**: Attackers send emails that appear to be from reputable organizations, such as banks or online services. These emails often contain urgent messages,

prompting the recipient to click on a link or download an attachment.

- **Example**: An email claiming to be from your bank, warning that your account has been compromised and urging you to click a link to reset your password.

2. **Spear Phishing:**

- **Description**: A more targeted form of phishing, where the attacker tailors the message to a specific individual or organization. This type of phishing is often highly personalized and may use information gathered from social media or other sources to appear more credible.

- **Example**: An email addressed directly to you, using your name and job title, asking you to review an attached document that appears to be work-related.

3. **Whaling:**

- **Description:** A type of spear phishing that targets high-profile individuals such as executives or high-ranking officials. The attackers aim to gain access to valuable corporate data or financial resources.

- **Example**: An email sent to a company's CEO, appearing to be from a trusted colleague, requesting an urgent wire transfer.

4. **Smishing (SMS Phishing):**

- **Description**: Phishing attempts carried out via text messages. These messages typically contain links to malicious websites or prompt the recipient to call a fraudulent phone number.

- **Example**: A text message claiming to be from your mobile carrier, stating that your bill is overdue and providing a link to make an immediate payment.

5. **Vishing (Voice Phishing):**

- **Description**: Phishing conducted over the phone, where attackers impersonate legitimate organizations and attempt to extract sensitive information directly from the victim.

- **Example**: A phone call from someone claiming to be from your credit card company, asking you to confirm your account details due to a supposed security breach.

How to Identify Phishing Scams
1. Check the Sender's Email Address or Phone Number:
- **What to Look For**: Phishing emails and messages often come from addresses or phone numbers that appear legitimate but contain slight variations or misspellings.

- **Action**: Always verify the sender's contact information before responding. If the email or message comes from an unknown or suspicious source, do not engage.

2. Look for Generic Greetings:
- **What to Look For**: Legitimate companies typically address you by name, while phishing attempts often use generic

greetings such as "Dear Customer" or "Dear User."

   - **Action**: Be cautious if an email or message does not address you by name or if the greeting feels impersonal.

3. Analyze the Content for Spelling and Grammar Errors:
   - **What to Look For**: Phishing emails frequently contain poor spelling, grammar mistakes, or awkward phrasing. These errors are often a sign of a fraudulent message.
   - **Action**: If you notice obvious errors in a message that claims to be from a reputable company, it's likely a phishing attempt. Avoid clicking on any links or downloading attachments.

4. Beware of Urgent or Threatening Language:
   - **What to Look For**: Phishing messages often create a sense of urgency, warning you of dire consequences if you don't act

immediately, such as account suspension or financial loss.

- **Action**: Legitimate organizations usually don't pressure you into immediate action. If you receive such a message, take the time to verify its authenticity before responding.

5. **Hover Over Links to Check the URL:**

- **What to Look For**: Phishing emails often contain links that appear to lead to legitimate websites but actually redirect you to a fake site designed to steal your information.

- **Action**: Before clicking on any link, hover your mouse over it to see the full URL. If the link doesn't match the expected destination or contains strange characters, don't click it.

6. **Avoid Suspicious Attachments:**

- **What to Look For**: Attachments in phishing emails may contain malware that can infect your device and steal your data.

- **Action**: Don't open any attachments unless you are certain of the sender's identity and the attachment's legitimacy. Be especially cautious with file types like .exe, .zip, or .doc.

Steps to Take If You Encounter a Phishing Attempt

1. Don't Click on Links or Download Attachments: If you suspect that an email or message is a phishing attempt, avoid interacting with any links or attachments.

2. Report the Phishing Attempt: Most companies have a designated email address where you can report phishing attempts (e.g., phishing@company.com). Reporting these scams helps organizations take action against cybercriminals.

3. Delete the Email or Message: Once reported, delete the suspicious email or message from your inbox to prevent accidental interaction.

4. Monitor Your Accounts: If you believe you've been targeted by a phishing scam,

keep a close eye on your financial accounts and credit reports for any unusual activity. Consider changing your passwords as a precaution.

By recognizing the signs of phishing and knowing how to respond, you can protect yourself from falling victim to these common but dangerous scams.

Creating Strong Passwords

Passwords are one of the most fundamental elements of cybersecurity. They serve as the first line of defense against unauthorized access to your accounts, devices, and personal information. Unfortunately, many people use weak passwords or reuse the same password across multiple accounts, making them vulnerable to cyber attacks. In this section, we will explore the importance of creating strong passwords and provide practical tips for managing them effectively.

Why Strong Passwords Matter

A strong password is your best defense against hackers trying to gain access to your accounts. Cybercriminals use various methods to crack passwords, from simple guessing to more sophisticated techniques like brute force attacks, where automated systems try every possible combination until they find the correct one. Weak passwords can be cracked in seconds, leaving your accounts and personal information exposed.

Characteristics of a Strong Password

1. **Length**: The longer the password, the more secure it is. Aim for at least 12 characters, though 16 or more is preferable.
2. **Complexity**: A strong password includes a mix of uppercase and lowercase letters, numbers, and special characters (e.g., @, #, $, !).
3. **Unpredictability**: Avoid using easily guessable information like your name, birthdate, or common words. Instead, opt

for random sequences or passphrases that are difficult to predict.

4. **Uniqueness**: Each account should have its own unique password to prevent a breach of one account from leading to the compromise of others.

Tips for Creating Strong Passwords
1. Use a Passphrase:
- **Description**: A passphrase is a series of random words or a sentence that is easy for you to remember but hard for others to guess. For example, "PurpleGiraffeDancesAtMidnight!" is a strong passphrase.

- **How to Implement**: Create a passphrase using unrelated words or a sentence that has personal significance to you. Ensure that it includes a mix of letters, numbers, and special characters.

2. Avoid Common Passwords:
- **Description**: Common passwords like "password123," "qwerty," or "123456" are

among the first that attackers will try when attempting to gain access to your accounts.

- **How to Implement**: Never use easily guessable passwords or variations of common passwords. Instead, opt for something unique and unpredictable.

3. **Use a Password Manager:**

- **Description**: A password manager is a tool that generates and stores complex, unique passwords for each of your accounts. This allows you to have strong passwords without needing to remember them all.

- **How to Implement**: Choose a reputable password manager, such as LastPass, 1Password, or Bitwarden. Use the password manager to generate and store passwords, and only remember the master password for accessing the manager.

4. **Enable Two-Factor Authentication (2FA):**

- **Description**: 2FA adds an extra layer of security by requiring a second form of verification, such as a code sent to your phone, in addition to your password.

- **How to Implement**: Whenever possible, enable 2FA on your accounts. This can be done through the account settings of most major online services. When 2FA is enabled, even if someone manages to obtain your password, they won't be able to access your account without the second factor of authentication.

5. Avoid Reusing Passwords:

- **Description**: Using the same password across multiple accounts exposes you to significant risk. If one account is compromised, all other accounts using that password are vulnerable.

- **How to Implement**: Always use a unique password for each account. This can be challenging to manage, which is why a password manager is invaluable. It helps generate and securely store different passwords for all your accounts, making it easier to maintain this best practice.

6. **Update Passwords Regularly**:
   - **Description**: Regularly changing your passwords minimizes the risk of long-term exposure, especially if one of your passwords has been compromised without your knowledge.
   - **How to Implement**: Set a schedule to update your passwords every three to six months. When creating new passwords, ensure they are as strong as the original and do not simply add or change a single character from the old password.

7. **Be Cautious with Security Questions:**
   - **Description**: Security questions are often used for account recovery, but the answers can sometimes be easily guessed or found through online searches.
   - **How to Implement**: Treat your answers to security questions like

passwords. Use random, unrelated answers and store them securely in your password manager. For example, if asked, "What is your mother's maiden name?" you might use a random string of characters or a completely unrelated word.

8. **Watch Out for Phishing Attempts:**
    - **Description**: Even the strongest password won't protect you if you inadvertently give it away through a phishing scam.
    - **How to Implement**: Be vigilant with any unsolicited requests for your password. Always verify the source of any such request, and never enter your password on a website without checking the URL to ensure it's legitimate.

Using a Password Manager

A password manager is an essential tool for anyone looking to enhance their online security. These tools not only generate and store strong passwords but also make it easier to use unique passwords across different accounts without the hassle of remembering them all.

1. **Choosing a Password Manager:**
    - **Considerations**: Look for a password manager with strong encryption, cross-platform support, and a user-friendly interface. Popular choices include LastPass, 1Password, Bitwarden, and Dashlane.
    - **Implementation**: After selecting a password manager, install it on your devices and create a master password. This should be the strongest password you've ever created because it grants access to all your other passwords.

2. **Storing and Managing Passwords:**
    - **Description**: Password managers can store hundreds of unique passwords, and many can also store secure notes, credit card information, and other sensitive data.

- **How to Implement**: Once your password manager is set up, start by entering all your current passwords. Then, update each account with a new, strong password generated by the manager. Over time, as you create new accounts or update existing ones, continue using the password manager to maintain strong, unique passwords across the board.

3. Using Autofill Features:
- **Description**: Many password managers offer an autofill feature that automatically enters your stored login credentials on websites and apps.
- **How to Implement**: Enable the autofill feature in your password manager's settings. This not only saves time but also ensures you always use the correct password, reducing the risk of phishing.

4. Backing Up Your Password Database:

- **Description**: Your password manager's database is critical, and losing it could mean losing access to all your accounts.

- **How to Implement**: Regularly back up your password database. Some password managers offer cloud backups, while others allow you to export your data securely. Make sure any backup is stored in a secure location, such as an encrypted USB drive.

5. Protecting Your Master Password:

- **Description**: The master password is the key to your password manager, so it must be extremely secure.

- **How to Implement**: Create a master password that is long, complex, and unique. Never reuse this password for any other account, and consider writing it down and storing it in a safe place, such as a secure, physical location known only to you.

By following these guidelines and utilizing a password manager, you significantly reduce the risk of unauthorized access to your online accounts and sensitive information.

Using Public Wi-Fi Safely

Public Wi-Fi networks are ubiquitous, offering convenient internet access in cafes, airports, hotels, and other public places. However, these networks are often unsecured and pose serious security risks. Cybercriminals can exploit public Wi-Fi to intercept data, distribute malware, and carry out man-in-the-middle attacks. Understanding the risks and adopting safe practices can help you stay secure while using public Wi-Fi.

Risks of Using Public Wi-Fi

1. **Unsecured Networks:**
    - **Description**: Many public Wi-Fi networks lack encryption, meaning data transmitted over the network can be easily intercepted by attackers.
    - **Risk**: Without encryption, any data you send or receive, including passwords, emails, and personal information, is

potentially exposed to anyone within range of the network.

2. **Man-in-the-Middle (MITM) Attacks:**

- **Description**: In a MITM attack, a cybercriminal intercepts communication between your device and the Wi-Fi network, allowing them to view, alter, or steal your data.

- **Risk**: Attackers can intercept login credentials, financial information, and other sensitive data, potentially leading to identity theft, financial loss, and unauthorized access to your accounts.

3. **Rogue Hotspots:**

- **Description**: Cybercriminals can set up fake Wi-Fi networks, known as rogue hotspots, that appear legitimate but are actually designed to steal your information.

- **Risk**: Connecting to a rogue hotspot can result in your data being captured and used for malicious purposes.

4. Malware Distribution:

- **Description**: Some public Wi-Fi networks may be compromised and used to distribute malware to connected devices.

- **Risk**: Malware can infect your device, leading to data breaches, system compromise, and further cyber attacks.

Tips for Using Public Wi-Fi Safely

1. Avoid Accessing Sensitive Information:

- **What to Do**: Refrain from accessing sensitive accounts, such as online banking or work email, while connected to public Wi-Fi.

- **Why It's Important**: Sensitive transactions are more vulnerable on unsecured networks. If you must access these accounts, consider using your mobile data or a secure network instead.

2. Use a Virtual Private Network (VPN):

- **What to Do**: A VPN encrypts your internet connection, making it much harder for attackers to intercept your data.

- **Why It's Important**: VPNs create a secure tunnel for your online activities, even on unsecured networks. Choose a reputable VPN service and activate it whenever you connect to public Wi-Fi.

3. Turn Off File Sharing and AirDrop:

- **What to Do:** Disable file sharing, AirDrop, and any other services that allow others to access your device.

- **Why It's Important**: These services can be exploited by attackers to gain unauthorized access to your device or files. Only enable them when necessary and in a secure environment.

4. Use HTTPS Websites:

- **What to Do**: Always check for "https://" at the beginning of a website's URL before entering any sensitive information.

- **Why It's Important**: HTTPS encrypts the data between your browser and the website, providing an additional layer of security. Avoid websites that only use HTTP, especially on public Wi-Fi.

5. Keep Your Software Updated:
- **What to Do**: Regularly update your operating system, browsers, and security software.

- **Why It's Important**: Updates often include security patches that protect against known vulnerabilities. Keeping your software up-to-date reduces the risk of exploitation.

6. Disable Auto-Connect Features:
- **What to Do**: Turn off auto-connect features that automatically connect your device to available Wi-Fi networks.

- **Why It's Important**: Auto-connect can inadvertently connect you to unsecured or rogue networks. Manually select trusted

Wi-Fi networks to ensure you're connecting to a legitimate source.

7. Log Out When Finished:
   - **What to Do:** Log out of any accounts you've accessed while on public Wi-Fi and close all browser windows.

   - **Why It's Important**: Logging out prevents unauthorized access to your accounts if your session information is intercepted.

8. Monitor Your Devices:
   - **What to Do**: Keep an eye on your devices and their activity while connected to public Wi-Fi. Be alert for any unusual behavior, such as pop-ups or unexpected disconnections.

   - **Why It's Important**: Early detection of suspicious activity can help you take action before significant damage is done, such as disconnecting from the network or running a malware scan.

When Public Wi-Fi is Unavoidable

Sometimes, using public Wi-Fi is necessary, especially when traveling or working remotely. In such cases, follow these additional precautions:

1. **Use a Personal Hotspot When Possible:**
   - **What to Do**: If you have a mobile data plan that allows it, use your smartphone as a personal hotspot instead of connecting to public Wi-Fi.
   - **Why It's Important**: Personal hotspots are generally more secure than public Wi-Fi, as they rely on your mobile carrier's network.

2. **Limit Your Activities:**
   - **What to Do**: Stick to low-risk activities, such as browsing news sites or checking the weather, when on public Wi-Fi.

- **Why It's Important**: Reducing the scope of your online activities minimizes the chances of exposing sensitive information.

3. Use Two-Factor Authentication (2FA):

- **What to Do**: Enable 2FA on your accounts, so even if your credentials are intercepted, the attacker cannot access your account without the second factor.

- **Why It's Important**: 2FA adds an extra layer of security, making it significantly harder for cybercriminals to access your accounts, even if they have obtained your password.

4. Pay Attention to Network Names:

- **What to Do:** Ensure you're connecting to the correct Wi-Fi network. Cybercriminals often set up rogue hotspots with names similar to legitimate networks (e.g., "Cafe_WiFi" vs. "CafeFreeWiFi").

- **Why It's Important**: Connecting to a rogue network can expose your data to attackers. Verify the network name with staff or signage before connecting.

5. Use Incognito Mode for Browsing:
   - **What to Do**: Use your browser's incognito or private browsing mode to reduce the amount of information stored on your device.
   - **Why It's Important**: Incognito mode prevents your browser from saving your browsing history, cookies, and form data, reducing the traces left behind after your session.

After Using Public Wi-Fi

Once you've finished using a public Wi-Fi network, there are a few steps you should take to ensure your security:

1. Disconnect from the Network:
   - **What to Do**: Always disconnect from the public Wi-Fi network once you're done using it.

- **Why It's Important**: Staying connected to a public Wi-Fi network when not in use increases the risk of an attacker gaining access to your device.

2. **Run a Security Scan:**
- **What to Do**: Use your device's antivirus or security software to perform a scan after using public Wi-Fi, checking for any malware or suspicious activity.
- **Why It's Important**: Early detection of malware can prevent more extensive damage to your device and data.

3. **Change Your Passwords if Necessary:**
- **What to Do**: If you suspect that your device was compromised while using public Wi-Fi, change the passwords of any accounts you accessed immediately.
- **Why It's Important**: Changing your passwords reduces the chances of cybercriminals using compromised credentials to access your accounts.

4. Monitor Account Activity:

- **What to Do**: Keep an eye on your financial accounts, email, and other sensitive accounts for any unusual activity following the use of public Wi-Fi.

- **Why It's Important**: Promptly detecting and reporting unauthorized transactions or account access can help mitigate the impact of a potential breach.

Safe internet practices are vital for protecting your personal information and maintaining your cybersecurity. By understanding how to recognize phishing scams, creating strong and unique passwords, and using public Wi-Fi safely, you can significantly reduce the risks associated with online activities. The strategies outlined in this chapter provide a foundation for navigating the internet securely, but staying informed and vigilant is key.

Chapter 4:

Protecting Your Online Identity

In today's interconnected world, your online identity is a crucial part of your personal and professional life. With increasing cyber threats, protecting your online identity is essential to safeguard your reputation, personal information, and financial security. This chapter provides comprehensive strategies for securing your online identity, focusing on social media security, email security, and the management of personal information.

Social Media Security

Social media platforms have become integral to our daily lives, providing a means to connect with friends, family, and professional networks. However, these platforms also pose significant risks if not properly secured. Cybercriminals often exploit social media accounts to steal personal information, launch phishing attacks, or impersonate users. To protect your online identity, it's essential to secure your social media accounts and manage your privacy settings effectively.

Securing Your Accounts

1. **Enable Two-Factor Authentication (2FA):**
    - **What to Do**: Activate two-factor authentication (2FA) on all your social media accounts. This feature requires you to provide a second form of identification (such as a code sent to your mobile device) in addition to your password when logging in.
   - **Why It's Important**: 2FA significantly enhances account security by adding an extra layer of protection. Even if someone

obtains your password, they would still need the second factor to access your account.

2. **Use Strong, Unique Passwords:**

- **What to Do**: Create strong, unique passwords for each of your social media accounts. Avoid using easily guessable information like birthdays or common words. Consider using a combination of letters, numbers, and special characters.

- **Why It's Important**: A strong, unique password reduces the likelihood of your account being compromised. If one account is hacked, using different passwords ensures that other accounts remain secure.

3. **Regularly Review Connected Apps:**

- **What to Do**: Periodically review the list of third-party apps and services connected to your social media accounts. Revoke access to any apps you no longer use or trust.

- **Why It's Important**: Third-party apps can be a weak link in your security chain. If one of these apps is compromised, it could provide attackers with access to your social media accounts.

4. **Monitor Account Activity:**

- **What to Do**: Regularly monitor your account activity, including login attempts, locations, and devices. Most social media platforms offer a security dashboard where you can review recent activity.

- **Why It's Important**: Monitoring your account activity allows you to quickly identify and respond to any suspicious behavior, such as unauthorized logins or unusual locations.

Managing Privacy Settings

1. **Adjust Your Privacy Settings:**

- **What to Do**: Review and adjust the privacy settings on your social media accounts to control who can see your posts, profile information, and friend list. Most platforms allow you to customize your settings for different audiences.

    - **Why It's Important**: Properly configured privacy settings limit who can view your personal information, reducing the risk of identity theft, stalking, or harassment.

2. Limit Profile Information:

    - **What to Do**: Be selective about the information you share on your social media profiles. Avoid including sensitive details such as your home address, phone number, or full birthdate.

    - **Why It's Important**: The less personal information you share, the less data cybercriminals have to exploit. Keeping sensitive details private helps protect you from identity theft and other online threats.

3. Be Cautious with Friend Requests:

    - **What to Do**: Only accept friend requests from people you know and trust. Be skeptical of requests from strangers or accounts with limited information.

- **Why It's Important**: Cybercriminals often create fake profiles to gain access to personal information or to spread malicious content. Accepting requests from unknown individuals increases your risk of exposure to these threats.

4. **Think Before You Post:**

- **What to Do**: Consider the potential impact of your posts before sharing them. Avoid posting sensitive information such as your location, travel plans, or financial details.

- **Why It's Important**: Once something is posted online, it can be difficult to remove. Oversharing can lead to various risks, including identity theft, burglary, or damage to your reputation.

Recognizing Social Media Threats

1. **Phishing Attempts:**
   - **What to Do**: Be aware of phishing attempts on social media, such as messages or posts asking for personal information or urging you to click on suspicious links.
   - **Why It's Important**: Phishing is a common tactic used by cybercriminals to steal personal information or credentials. Recognizing and avoiding these attempts is key to protecting your accounts.

2. **Malicious Links and Content:**
   - **What to Do**: Be cautious when clicking on links or downloading content from social media, especially if it's from an unknown source.
   - **Why It's Important**: Cybercriminals often use social media to distribute malware or direct users to malicious websites. Ensuring that you only engage with trusted content helps keep your devices and accounts secure.

3. **Impersonation and Identity Theft:**

- **What to Do**: If you notice a fake profile pretending to be you or someone you know, report it to the platform immediately.

- **Why It's Important**: Impersonation is a serious threat that can lead to reputation damage or fraud. Promptly reporting fake profiles helps protect your identity and the identities of others.

Email Security

Email remains one of the most widely used forms of communication, making it a prime target for cybercriminals. Securing your email accounts and practicing safe email habits are essential steps in protecting your online identity.

Securing Your Email Accounts

1. Enable Two-Factor Authentication (2FA):

- **What to Do**: Enable 2FA on your email accounts, requiring a secondary form of authentication in addition to your password.

- **Why It's Important**: 2FA adds an additional layer of security, making it more difficult for unauthorized users to gain access to your email, even if they obtain your password.

2. **Set Strong, Unique Passwords**:

- **What to Do**: Use strong, unique passwords for your email accounts. Avoid using the same password across multiple accounts.

- **Why It's Important**: A strong, unique password helps protect your email from being hacked. If one account is compromised, other accounts with different passwords remain secure.

3. **Be Mindful of Security Questions:**

- **What to Do**: Choose security questions with answers that are difficult to guess.

Consider using unrelated answers stored securely in a password manager.

   - **Why It's Important**: Security questions can be exploited if the answers are easily accessible. Strengthening them helps secure your account recovery options.

4. Monitor Account Activity:

   - **What to Do**: Regularly check the login history and activity on your email account for any unusual access or locations.

   - **Why It's Important**: Unusual activity can indicate that your account has been compromised, allowing you to take swift action to secure it.

Practicing Safe Email Habits

1. Avoid Opening Suspicious Emails:

   - **What to Do**: Be cautious about opening emails from unknown senders or those with suspicious subject lines or attachments.

   - **Why It's Important**: Suspicious emails often contain phishing attempts or malware that can compromise your email account or device.

2. **Do Not Click on Unknown Links:**

- **What to Do**: Hover over links to verify their destination before clicking, and avoid clicking on links in emails from unfamiliar sources.

- **Why It's Important**: Phishing links can direct you to fake websites designed to steal your login credentials or install malware on your device.

3. **Be Wary of Email Attachments:**

- **What to Do**: Only open attachments from trusted sources, and scan them with antivirus software before opening.

- **Why It's Important**: Malicious attachments are a common method of delivering malware, which can compromise your device and steal your personal information.

4. Use Encryption for Sensitive Emails:

- **What to Do:** When sending sensitive information via email, use encryption to protect the contents from being intercepted.

- **Why It's Important**: Encryption ensures that only the intended recipient can read the email, safeguarding your personal information during transmission.

Avoiding Spam and Scams

1. Do Not Respond to Spam Emails:

- **What to Do**: If you receive a spam email, delete it without responding. Do not click any links or provide any information.

- **Why It's Important**: Responding to spam can confirm to the sender that your email address is active, leading to more spam or targeted scams.

2. Report Phishing Attempts:

- **What to Do**: Most email providers have a feature to report phishing attempts. Use this feature to help protect yourself and others.

- **Why It's Important**: Reporting phishing emails helps your provider filter them out in the future, reducing your risk of falling victim to similar scams.

3. Unsubscribe from Unwanted Emails:

- **What to Do**: Use the unsubscribe link at the bottom of legitimate emails to remove yourself from mailing lists you no longer wish to be part of.

- **Why It's Important**: Unsubscribing reduces the clutter in your inbox and minimizes your exposure to potential phishing or scam emails.

Managing Personal Information

Your personal information is valuable, both to you and to cybercriminals. Protecting this information online is crucial to prevent identity theft, financial fraud, and other malicious activities. Here's how you can manage your personal information more securely.

Limiting the Sharing of Sensitive Data

1. Be Selective with Information You Share Online:

- **What to Do**: Only provide personal information on trusted websites and to reputable organizations. Avoid sharing sensitive details like your Social Security number, full birthdate, or financial information unless absolutely necessary.

- **Why It's Important**: The less information you share, the lower your risk of identity theft or data breaches. Be cautious about who you trust with your data. Every piece of information you share can be used by cybercriminals to build a profile, which can be exploited for various malicious purposes.

2. Use Privacy Controls:

- **What to Do**: Utilize privacy controls offered by websites, apps, and social media platforms to limit who can access your personal information. Regularly review these settings to ensure they align with your current privacy preferences.

- **Why It's Important**: Privacy controls give you more control over your personal information, allowing you to decide who can see what. This minimizes the chances of your information being accessed by unauthorized parties.

3. Limit What You Share on Social Media:

- **What to Do**: Be mindful of the personal details you post on social media. Avoid sharing information that could be used to identify you, such as your location, travel plans, or details about your family.

- **Why It's Important**: Cybercriminals often use social media to gather information about potential targets. By limiting what you share, you reduce the amount of information available for exploitation.

4. Review and Manage Permissions for Apps and Services:

- **What to Do**: Regularly review the permissions you've granted to apps and services, especially those that have access to your location, contacts, or other personal data. Revoke permissions that are not essential for the app's function.

- **Why It's Important**: Apps with excessive permissions can collect and share more data than necessary, increasing your risk of privacy violations. By managing permissions, you can better control how your data is used.

Safeguarding Your Personal Data

1. Use Strong Security Questions:

- **What to Do**: Choose security questions and answers that are not easily guessable or found online. Consider using unrelated answers stored securely in a password manager.

- **Why It's Important**: Weak security questions can be exploited by attackers to gain access to your accounts. Strengthening them helps protect your account recovery options.

2. Minimize Sharing Personal Information with Third Parties:

- **What to Do**: Avoid sharing personal information with third-party services or websites unless absolutely necessary. When you do share information, ensure that the service has a strong privacy policy and data protection practices.

- **Why It's Important**: Sharing personal information with third parties increases the risk of that data being leaked, sold, or misused. Ensuring that only reputable and necessary services have access to your data reduces this risk.

3. Monitor Your Financial Statements:

- **What to Do**: Regularly review your bank and credit card statements for unauthorized transactions. Consider setting up alerts for any unusual activity.

- **Why It's Important**: Early detection of unauthorized activity can help you respond quickly to potential identity theft or financial fraud. Monitoring your financial statements is a crucial step in protecting your financial identity.

4. Be Cautious with Data Sharing in Public or Shared Spaces:

- **What to Do**: Avoid accessing sensitive accounts or sharing personal information on public or shared devices. If you must, ensure that you log out completely and clear any browsing data.

- **Why It's Important**: Public or shared devices may have weak security, increasing the risk of your data being intercepted or accessed by others. Taking precautions when using these devices helps safeguard your personal information.

5. Use Encryption and Secure Communication Channels:

- **What to Do**: When sharing sensitive information online, use encrypted communication channels such as secure messaging apps or websites that use HTTPS. Consider using email encryption for particularly sensitive data.

- **Why It's Important**: Encryption protects your data by making it unreadable to anyone who intercepts it. Using secure communication channels ensures that your personal information remains private during transmission.

Responding to Data Breaches

1. Monitor for Data Breaches:

- **What to Do**: Use services like Have I Been Pwned to check if your information has been exposed in a data breach. Set up alerts to be notified if your information is compromised.

- **Why It's Important**: Monitoring for data breaches allows you to take prompt action to secure your accounts if your information is exposed. Early detection is key to minimizing the damage of a breach.

2. Respond Quickly to Data Breaches:
- **What to Do**: If you discover that your information has been compromised in a data breach, immediately change your passwords, especially for any accounts using the same password as the breached service. Consider enabling 2FA on those accounts if you haven't already.
- **Why It's Important**: Acting quickly can prevent cybercriminals from using your compromised information to access other accounts or commit identity theft. Prompt response is critical in mitigating the effects of a data breach.

3. Notify Affected Parties:
- **What to Do**: If your personal information is stolen and could affect others

(e.g., if your email is hacked and used to send phishing emails), notify those who might be impacted.

   - **Why It's Important**: By notifying affected parties, you help prevent further spread of the breach and protect others from falling victim to fraud or identity theft.

4. **Consider Freezing Your Credit:**

   - **What to Do**: If you believe your financial information has been compromised, consider placing a freeze on your credit report with the major credit bureaus (Equifax, Experian, and TransUnion).

   - **Why It's Important**: Freezing your credit makes it more difficult for identity thieves to open new accounts in your name, protecting you from financial fraud.

Protecting your online identity requires vigilance, proactive measures, and a clear understanding of the risks involved.

Chapter 5:

Data Protection and Privacy

Data protection and privacy are paramount in today's digital landscape, where data breaches, cyberattacks, and unauthorized surveillance are increasingly common. Understanding how to safeguard your data and protect your privacy is essential for both individuals and organizations. This chapter will delve into the importance of data backups, the fundamentals of encryption, and the various privacy tools available to help you maintain control over your personal information.

Importance of Backups

Data loss can occur due to various reasons, such as hardware failure, accidental deletion, ransomware attacks, or natural disasters. To mitigate the impact of data loss, regular backups are essential. Backups ensure that you have a copy of your important data stored securely, allowing you to recover it in case of an emergency. Here, we will explore the importance of backups, different backup methods, and best practices for ensuring your data is always safe.

Why Backups Matter

1. **Protection Against Data Loss:**

- **What to Do**: Regularly back up your data to protect against potential data loss caused by hardware failures, accidental deletions, or cyberattacks.

- **Why It's Important**: Backups are your last line of defense in case of data loss. Without backups, recovering lost or compromised data can be nearly impossible, leading to significant disruptions in your personal or professional life.

2. Mitigation of Ransomware Threats:

- **What to Do**: Keep backups of your data that are not connected to your primary network or systems, such as offline or cloud backups.

- **Why It's Important**: Ransomware attacks can encrypt your data and demand payment for its release. Having an up-to-date backup allows you to restore your data without paying the ransom, thereby reducing the impact of such attacks.

3. Business Continuity:

- **What to Do**: For businesses, implement a backup strategy as part of your disaster recovery plan to ensure continuity of operations in the event of data loss.

- **Why It's Important**: Businesses rely heavily on data for their operations. Regular backups ensure that critical business data can be restored quickly, minimizing downtime and financial losses.

Types of Backups

1. Full Backups:
- **What to Do**: A full backup involves copying all the data from your system to a secure storage location. This method is typically used as the first backup in a backup strategy.
- **Why It's Important**: Full backups provide a complete copy of all your data, making them the most comprehensive backup method. They are essential for restoring systems to a previous state in case of major data loss.

2. Incremental Backups:
- **What to Do**: Incremental backups only save the changes made since the last backup (either full or incremental), reducing the amount of data that needs to be stored.
- **Why It's Important**: Incremental backups are faster and use less storage space than full backups. They are ideal for frequent backups, allowing you to maintain

up-to-date copies of your data without excessive storage requirements.

3. **Differential Backups:**
   - **What to Do**: A differential backup saves all the data that has changed since the last full backup, making it a middle ground between full and incremental backups.
   - **Why It's Important**: Differential backups provide a balance between the speed and storage efficiency of incremental backups and the comprehensiveness of full backups. They are useful for regular backups without needing to perform a full backup each time.

4. **Cloud Backups:**
   - **What to Do**: Cloud backups involve storing your data on remote servers managed by a cloud service provider, allowing you to access your data from any location.
   - **Why It's Important**: Cloud backups offer convenience and security by

automatically saving your data offsite, protecting it from physical damage or theft. They also provide easy access to your data from different devices and locations.

5. Local Backups:

- **What to Do**: Local backups involve storing your data on physical devices such as external hard drives, USB drives, or network-attached storage (NAS).

- **Why It's Important**: Local backups provide quick access to your data and are not reliant on an internet connection. However, they must be stored securely to protect against physical theft or damage.

Best Practices for Backups

1. Follow the 3-2-1 Rule:

- **What to Do**: The 3-2-1 rule suggests keeping three copies of your data: two on different storage devices and one offsite (such as in the cloud).

- **Why It's Important**: This rule provides redundancy, ensuring that even if one copy is lost or corrupted, you have other backups available. The offsite backup protects against physical disasters like fire or flooding.

2. Automate Your Backups:
- **What to Do**: Use automated backup software to schedule regular backups without manual intervention. Set it up to back up your data daily, weekly, or monthly, depending on your needs.
- **Why It's Important**: Automated backups reduce the risk of forgetting to perform a backup, ensuring that your data is always protected. Regular backups also minimize the amount of data lost in case of an incident.

3. Test Your Backups:
- **What to Do**: Periodically test your backups to ensure that they are functioning

correctly and that you can restore your data when needed.

- **Why It's Important**: Testing your backups verifies that they are reliable and that the data can be successfully recovered. This step is crucial in avoiding surprises during an actual data loss event.

4. **Secure Your Backups:**

- **What to Do**: Encrypt your backups and store them in secure locations. For physical backups, consider using a safe or other secure storage.

- **Why It's Important**: Unencrypted or unsecured backups are vulnerable to theft, unauthorized access, or tampering. Encrypting your backups protects your data from being accessed by unauthorized parties.

Understanding Encryption

Encryption is one of the most powerful tools available for protecting your data. It converts your information into a code that can only be decoded by someone with the correct key. Encryption ensures that even if your data is intercepted, it remains unreadable to unauthorized users. This section will explain the basics of encryption and how you can use it to protect your data.

What is Encryption?

1. Basic Explanation:

- **What It Is**: Encryption is a process that converts plaintext (readable data) into ciphertext (unreadable code) using an algorithm and an encryption key.

- **How It Works**: When you encrypt data, the algorithm uses the key to scramble the data into a form that cannot be understood without the corresponding decryption key. To access the original data, the correct key must be used to decrypt the ciphertext back into plaintext.

- **Why It's Important**: Encryption protects your data from unauthorized access. Even if someone intercepts your encrypted data, they cannot read it without the decryption key. This makes encryption a vital tool for securing sensitive information.

2. Types of Encryption:

- **Symmetric Encryption**: This method uses the same key for both encryption and decryption. It is faster and more efficient but requires the secure sharing of the key between parties.

- **Asymmetric Encryption**: This method uses a pair of keys—one for encryption (public key) and one for decryption (private key). It is more secure but slower than symmetric encryption and is often used for secure communications like email.

How to Use Encryption Tools

1. File and Disk Encryption:

- **What to Do**: Use encryption software to protect sensitive files or entire hard drives. Popular tools include BitLocker for Windows, FileVault for Mac, and VeraCrypt for cross-platform use.

- **Why It's Important**: Encrypting files or disks ensures that even if your computer or storage device is lost or stolen, the data remains protected. Without the decryption key, the encrypted files cannot be accessed.

2. Email Encryption:

- **What to Do**: Use email encryption tools like PGP (Pretty Good Privacy) or S/MIME (Secure/Multipurpose Internet Mail Extensions) to encrypt your email communications.

- **Why It's Important**: Email encryption protects the contents of your emails from being read by anyone other than the intended recipient. It is especially important when sending sensitive information.

3. Encrypting Cloud Storage:
- **What to Do**: Use cloud storage services that offer encryption, or encrypt your files before uploading them to the cloud. Services like Tresorit and Sync.com provide end-to-end encryption.

- **Why It's Important**: Encrypting data in the cloud protects it from being accessed by unauthorized parties, including the cloud service provider. End-to-end encryption ensures that only you and those you authorize can access your files.

4. Using Encrypted Messaging Apps:
- **What to Do**: Use messaging apps that offer end-to-end encryption, such as Signal or WhatsApp, to protect your communications from being intercepted.

- **Why It's Important**: Encrypted messaging apps ensure that only you and the person you're communicating with can read your messages. This protects your privacy and secures your conversations from eavesdroppers.

Best Practices for Encryption

1. Keep Your Encryption Keys Secure:

- **What to Do**: Store your encryption keys in a secure location, such as a password manager or a hardware security module (HSM).

- **Why It's Important**: The security of your encrypted data depends on the protection of your encryption keys. If your keys are compromised, the encrypted data can be decrypted and accessed by unauthorized parties.

2. Regularly Update Encryption Tools:

- **What to Do**: Ensure that the encryption tools you use are up-to-date with the latest security patches and improvements. This applies to both software-based encryption tools and hardware that supports encryption.

- **Why It's Important**: Outdated encryption software may contain vulnerabilities that can be exploited by cybercriminals. Keeping your tools updated ensures that you are using the most secure versions available, providing better protection for your data.

3. Use Strong Encryption Algorithms:

- **What to Do**: When configuring encryption, choose strong, widely recognized algorithms like AES (Advanced Encryption Standard) with 256-bit keys.

- **Why It's Important**: Strong encryption algorithms provide a higher level of security, making it more difficult for attackers to crack the encryption. AES-256, for example, is considered highly secure and is widely used in both government and private sectors.

4. Avoid Reusing Encryption Keys:

- **What to Do**: Use unique encryption keys for different files, devices, or communications. Avoid reusing the same key across multiple platforms or services.
   - **Why It's Important**: Reusing encryption keys increases the risk that if one key is compromised, multiple pieces of data could be decrypted. Using unique keys for different purposes limits the potential damage of a key compromise.

Privacy Tools

In addition to encryption, there are various privacy tools designed to protect your online activities and personal information from prying eyes. These tools include Virtual Private Networks (VPNs), secure browsers, and privacy-focused apps. This section provides an overview of these tools and how they can be used to enhance your online privacy.

Virtual Private Networks (VPNs)

1. What is a VPN?

- **What It Is**: A VPN is a service that encrypts your internet connection and routes it through a server in a location of your choice. This masks your IP address and makes your online activities more difficult to trace.

- **How It Works**: When you connect to a VPN, your internet traffic is encrypted and sent to the VPN server. The server then forwards your requests to the destination website or service, masking your IP address with that of the server. The responses are sent back to the VPN server, which decrypts them and sends them to you.

- **Why It's Important**: VPNs provide privacy by preventing your internet service provider (ISP), government, or hackers from monitoring your online activities. They also help bypass geographic restrictions, allowing you to access content that may be blocked in your region.

2. Choosing a VPN Service:

- **What to Do**: When selecting a VPN, look for services that offer strong encryption, a no-logs policy, and servers in multiple locations. Popular choices include NordVPN, ExpressVPN, and ProtonVPN.

- **Why It's Important**: Not all VPNs offer the same level of privacy and security. A no-logs policy ensures that the VPN provider does not keep records of your activities, while strong encryption protects your data from being intercepted.

3. Best Practices for Using a VPN:

- **What to Do**: Always connect to your VPN before accessing sensitive information or using public Wi-Fi. Enable the VPN's kill switch feature, which disconnects your internet if the VPN connection drops, preventing your data from being exposed.

- **Why It's Important**: Using a VPN consistently enhances your online privacy, especially on untrusted networks. The kill switch feature ensures that your data remains encrypted even if the VPN connection is interrupted.

Secure Browsers

1. What is a Secure Browser?

- **What It Is**: A secure browser is designed to protect your privacy by minimizing the data collected about your browsing habits. It includes features like blocking trackers, disabling third-party cookies, and preventing fingerprinting.

- **How It Works**: Secure browsers, such as Firefox with privacy settings enabled, Brave, or Tor Browser, actively block tracking scripts and ads that collect data about your browsing. Tor Browser also routes your traffic through multiple servers (nodes) in the Tor network, anonymizing your IP address and location.

- **Why It's Important**: Standard browsers often collect significant amounts of data about your online activities, which can be used to track you across the web. Secure browsers reduce this data collection, providing a higher level of privacy.

2. **Using Private Browsing Modes:**

- **What to Do**: Most browsers offer a private or incognito mode that doesn't save your browsing history or cookies. Use this mode when you don't want your activities stored on your device.

- **Why It's Important**: While private browsing modes don't make you completely anonymous, they help prevent your activities from being recorded on your device, which is useful when using shared or public computers.

3. **Additional Privacy Extensions:**

- **What to Do**: Enhance your browser's privacy features with extensions like uBlock Origin (ad and tracker blocker), HTTPS Everywhere (forces HTTPS connections), and Privacy Badger (blocks invisible trackers).

- **Why It's Important**: These extensions add an extra layer of protection by blocking ads, trackers, and unsecured connections, further reducing the amount of data that websites can collect about you.

Privacy-Focused Apps

1. Encrypted Messaging Apps:
- **What to Do**: Use messaging apps that offer end-to-end encryption, such as Signal, WhatsApp, or Telegram (for secret chats).
- **Why It's Important**: Encrypted messaging apps ensure that only you and the recipient can read the messages, protecting your conversations from being intercepted or accessed by third parties.

2. Secure Email Services:
- **What to Do**: Choose email services that prioritize privacy, such as ProtonMail or Tutanota, which offer end-to-end encryption for your emails.

- **Why It's Important**: Traditional email services often lack robust encryption, leaving your emails vulnerable to being read by service providers or hackers. Secure email services provide encryption, ensuring that only you and the recipient can access the content of your emails.

3. **Password Managers:**
   - **What to Do**: Use a password manager to store and generate strong, unique passwords for each of your online accounts. Examples include LastPass, 1Password, and Bitwarden.
   - **Why It's Important**: Password managers securely store your passwords in an encrypted vault, reducing the risk of password reuse and making it easier to maintain strong security across multiple accounts.

4. **Privacy-Focused Search Engines:**
   - **What to Do**: Use search engines that do not track your searches, such as

DuckDuckGo or Startpage, instead of traditional search engines that collect and store your data.

 - **Why It's Important**: Privacy-focused search engines protect your search history from being tracked and used to build a profile of your interests and activities, offering a more private browsing experience.

Data protection and privacy are crucial aspects of cybersecurity that require both awareness and proactive measures. By understanding the importance of regular data backups, using encryption to protect sensitive information, and utilizing privacy tools like VPNs, secure browsers, and privacy-focused apps, you can significantly enhance your digital security. As cyber threats continue to evolve, maintaining control over your data and privacy is more important than ever.

Chapter 6:

Responding to Cyber Threats

In an increasingly connected world, the likelihood of encountering cyber threats is higher than ever. Knowing how to respond effectively to these threats is crucial in minimizing damage, recovering lost data, and preventing future incidents. This chapter will guide you through the steps to take if your accounts or devices are compromised, how to report cybercrime, and the best practices for recovering from cyber attacks.

What to Do in Case of a Breach

A breach occurs when unauthorized individuals gain access to your data or systems. This could be through hacking, phishing, malware, or other malicious activities. The immediate steps you take following a breach can significantly affect the extent of the damage and your ability to recover.

1. Identify the Breach
The first step in responding to a breach is to identify it. This can sometimes be obvious, such as when you receive a notification of a login attempt from an unfamiliar location, or it can be subtle, such as noticing unusual activity on your accounts.

- **Monitor Your Accounts**: Regularly check your bank statements, social media accounts, and email for any suspicious activity. Look out for unauthorized transactions, changes in account settings, or unfamiliar devices logged into your accounts.

- **Check for Signs of Malware**: If your device is behaving strangely—such as running slowly, crashing frequently, or displaying pop-up ads—it could be infected with malware. Use an antivirus program to scan for and remove any malicious software.

- **Review Access Logs**: If you have access to logs (such as in a business setting), review them for any unusual activity, such as logins from unfamiliar IP addresses or unauthorized access to sensitive data.

2. **Contain the Breach**
Once you've identified that a breach has occurred, your next priority should be to contain it. This involves preventing the attacker from causing further harm and securing any compromised systems or accounts.

- **Disconnect from the Internet**: If you suspect that your device is compromised, disconnect it from the internet immediately. This prevents the attacker from continuing to access your system or spreading the infection to other devices.

- **Change Passwords**: Change the passwords for any compromised accounts immediately. If you use the same password across multiple sites, change those as well. Use strong, unique passwords for each account, and consider using a password manager to generate and store them securely.

- **Enable Two-Factor Authentication (2FA)**: If you haven't already, enable 2FA on all your accounts. This adds an extra layer of security by requiring a second form of verification (such as a text message code) in addition to your password.

- **Revoke Unauthorized Access**: If someone has gained access to your accounts, revoke their access immediately. This can involve logging out of all sessions, removing unfamiliar devices, and resetting security questions.

3. Assess the Damage

After containing the breach, assess the extent of the damage. Understanding what information has been compromised will help you determine the next steps and any additional actions that may be required.

- **Determine What Was Accessed**: Identify what data or systems were accessed during the breach. This could include personal information, financial details, business documents, or customer data.

- **Identify the Source of the Breach**: Try to determine how the breach occurred. Was it through a phishing email, weak password, unpatched software, or something else? Understanding the source of the breach can help you prevent similar incidents in the future.

- **Check for Data Exfiltration**: If sensitive data was accessed, check to see if it was copied or sent outside of your network.

This could indicate that your data has been exfiltrated (stolen) by the attacker.

4. Secure Your Systems

Once the breach has been contained and assessed, take steps to secure your systems and prevent future incidents.

- **Update Software and Firmware**: Ensure that all your software and devices are updated with the latest security patches. This includes your operating system, antivirus software, applications, and router firmware.

- **Remove Malware**: If the breach involved malware, use a reputable antivirus program to remove any malicious software from your devices. Follow up with a full system scan to ensure that your system is clean.

- **Strengthen Security Measures**: Review and enhance your security measures. This could involve implementing stronger access controls, improving network security, or educating yourself and others about safe online practices.

5. Notify Affected Parties

If the breach has resulted in the compromise of sensitive information, you may need to notify affected parties, such as customers, employees, or partners.

- **Inform Affected Individuals**: If personal information was compromised, inform the affected individuals as soon as possible. Provide them with information on what was accessed and what steps they should take to protect themselves, such as changing passwords or monitoring their accounts for suspicious activity.

- **Follow Legal Requirements**: Depending on your location and the nature of the breach, you may be legally required to report the incident to regulatory authorities or notify individuals whose data was compromised. Ensure you understand and comply with any relevant laws or regulations.

Reporting Cybercrime

Reporting cybercrime is an important step in holding perpetrators accountable and preventing further incidents. Cybercrime can include hacking, identity theft, online fraud, and other illegal activities conducted over the internet.

1. **When to Report Cybercrime**
Not every cybersecurity incident requires reporting, but serious breaches, financial losses, or incidents involving illegal activities should be reported to the appropriate authorities.

- **Serious Breaches**: If the breach involves the theft of personal information, financial data, or sensitive business information, it should be reported. This is particularly important if it could lead to identity theft or financial loss.

- **Financial Losses**: If you have suffered financial losses due to a cyber attack, such as through online fraud or theft of funds, report the incident to your bank and local law enforcement.

- **Illegal Activities**: If the incident involves illegal activities, such as hacking, cyberstalking, or distributing illegal content, report it to the authorities immediately.

2. **How to Report Cybercrime**
Reporting cybercrime involves contacting the appropriate authorities and providing them with the necessary information to investigate the incident.

- **Contact Law Enforcement**: Report the incident to your local law enforcement agency or a specialized cybercrime unit. In some countries, you can also report cybercrime to national agencies like the FBI's Internet Crime Complaint Center (IC3) in the United States or Action Fraud in the UK.

- **Notify Relevant Organizations**: If the breach involves financial institutions or online services, notify them immediately. This could include your bank, credit card company, or the service provider affected by the breach.

- **Document the Incident**: Provide as much detail as possible about the incident, including when it occurred, how it happened, and any evidence you have (such as suspicious emails, screenshots, or logs). This will assist authorities in their investigation.

- **Use Online Reporting Tools**: Many countries offer online tools or websites where you can report cybercrime. For example, the FBI's IC3 allows you to submit complaints online, and Europol provides resources for reporting cybercrime in Europe.

3. Protecting Yourself After Reporting
After reporting cybercrime, take additional steps to protect yourself and prevent further incidents.

- **Monitor Your Accounts**: Keep a close eye on your financial accounts, credit reports, and online accounts for any suspicious activity. If you notice anything unusual, report it immediately.

- **Consider Identity Theft Protection**: If your personal information was compromised, consider signing up for an identity theft protection service. These services monitor your information and alert you to potential misuse.

- **Stay Informed**: Keep up-to-date with the latest cybersecurity news and trends. Knowing about new threats and vulnerabilities can help you stay ahead of potential risks.

Recovering from Cyber Attacks

Recovering from a cyber attack can be a challenging process, but taking the right steps can help you minimize the damage and restore your systems.

1. **Restore Your Data**
If the attack resulted in data loss or corruption, restoring your data from backups should be one of your top priorities.

- **Use Backups**: If you have backups of your data, use them to restore your system to a state before the attack occurred. Ensure that your backups are clean and free of malware before restoring them.

- **Consult with Experts**: If you're unsure how to restore your data or if the situation is complex, consider consulting with cybersecurity professionals who can guide you through the recovery process.

2. Strengthen Your Defenses
After recovering from an attack, it's crucial to strengthen your defenses to prevent future incidents.

- **Review and Update Security Policies**: If the attack exposed weaknesses in your security policies or procedures, review and update them to address those gaps.

- **Educate Yourself and Others**: Ensure that you and others who may have access to your systems are educated about cybersecurity best practices. This includes recognizing phishing attempts, using strong passwords, and staying vigilant for potential threats.

- **Implement Advanced Security Measures**: Consider implementing more advanced security measures, such as multi-factor authentication, intrusion detection systems, or network segmentation.

3. Learn from the Incident
Every cyber attack presents an opportunity to learn and improve your defenses.

- **Conduct a Post-Incident Review**: Analyze the attack to understand how it happened and what could have been done differently. Identify the root cause and implement changes to prevent a similar incident in the future.

- **Update Your Incident Response Plan**: If you don't have an incident response plan, create one. If you do, update it based on the lessons learned from the attack. A well-prepared response plan can make a significant difference in minimizing damage during future incidents.

- **Stay Resilient**: Cyber attacks can be disruptive and stressful, but it's important to stay resilient. Building a strong cybersecurity foundation and learning from past incidents will better equip you to handle future threats.

Responding to cyber threats requires a proactive and well-informed approach. By knowing what steps to take in the event of a breach, understanding how to report cybercrime, and effectively recovering from cyber attacks, you can minimize the impact of these incidents and strengthen your overall cybersecurity posture. Cyber threats are a persistent risk, but with the right knowledge and tools, you can protect yourself and your data from harm.

Chapter 7:

Building a Cybersecurity Routine

Cybersecurity is not a one-time effort but an ongoing process that requires continuous attention and adaptation. To effectively protect yourself and your digital assets, it's essential to develop a routine that incorporates regular security checks, staying informed about the latest threats, and implementing a personal cybersecurity plan. This chapter will guide you through the steps to build a robust cybersecurity routine that can help safeguard your data and online presence.

Regular Security Checks

Regularly checking and updating your security settings is a foundational aspect of maintaining a secure digital environment.

Just as you would regularly change the locks on your doors or check the batteries in your smoke detectors, your digital security also requires periodic maintenance to stay effective.

1. **Review and Update Passwords**

Passwords are your first line of defense against unauthorized access to your accounts. However, passwords can become vulnerable over time, especially if they are reused or weak.

- **Change Passwords Regularly**: Aim to change your passwords every three to six months, particularly for critical accounts such as your email, banking, and social media accounts. Avoid reusing passwords across multiple sites, as this increases the risk of a widespread breach if one password is compromised.

- **Use Strong, Unique Passwords**: Ensure your passwords are long, complex, and unique for each account. A strong password typically includes a mix of uppercase and lowercase letters, numbers, and special characters. Consider using a passphrase—a sequence of random words that are easier to remember but hard to guess.

- **Utilize a Password Manager**: A password manager can help you generate, store, and manage strong, unique passwords for all your accounts. This tool encrypts your passwords and stores them securely, so you only need to remember one master password.

2. **Update Software and Firmware**

Software and firmware updates often include patches for security vulnerabilities that could be exploited by hackers. Keeping your devices and applications up-to-date is critical for maintaining security.

- **Enable Automatic Updates**: Whenever possible, enable automatic updates for your operating system, antivirus software, applications, and any other critical software. This ensures that you receive the latest security patches as soon as they are available.

- **Manually Check for Updates**: For software that does not offer automatic updates, regularly check for updates manually. This includes firmware updates for devices such as routers, smart home devices, and IoT gadgets.

- **Uninstall Unused Software**: Remove any software or applications that you no longer use. Unused software can become outdated and vulnerable to attacks, posing a risk to your system.

3. Monitor Account Activity

Keeping an eye on your account activity can help you quickly detect and respond to unauthorized access or suspicious behavior.

- **Check Account Activity Logs**: Many online services, such as email providers and social media platforms, allow you to view recent account activity, including logins from different devices or locations. Regularly review these logs to ensure that only authorized access has occurred.

- **Set Up Alerts**: Enable account alerts that notify you of important actions, such as logins from new devices, password changes, or unusual transactions. These alerts can help you detect and respond to potential breaches more quickly.

- **Review Financial Statements**: Regularly review your bank and credit card statements for any unauthorized transactions. Promptly report any suspicious activity to your financial institution.

4. Perform Regular Backups

Regular backups are essential for protecting your data against loss due to cyber attacks, hardware failures, or accidental deletion.

- **Schedule Automatic Backups**: Set up automatic backups for your important files and data. Ensure that backups are stored in a secure location, such as an external hard drive or a cloud storage service that offers encryption.

- **Verify Backup Integrity**: Periodically check that your backups are complete and that the data can be restored successfully. This ensures that your backup strategy is effective and that you can rely on it in case of an emergency.

Staying Informed

The cybersecurity landscape is constantly evolving, with new threats emerging regularly. Staying informed about the latest trends and best practices is crucial for maintaining strong security.

1. Follow Reputable Cybersecurity News Sources

Subscribing to reputable cybersecurity news sources can help you stay updated on the latest threats, vulnerabilities, and security practices.

- **Cybersecurity Blogs and Websites**: Follow well-known cybersecurity blogs and websites, such as Krebs on Security, Naked Security by Sophos, and the SANS Internet Storm Center. These sources provide timely updates on emerging threats and expert advice on protecting your systems.

- **Industry Reports and Bulletins**: Many cybersecurity organizations and companies publish regular reports and bulletins that provide insights into current trends and vulnerabilities. For example, the Verizon Data Breach Investigations Report (DBIR) offers an annual overview of the state of cybersecurity.

- **Government and Nonprofit Resources**: Government agencies, such as the U.S. Cybersecurity and Infrastructure Security Agency (CISA), and nonprofit organizations, like the Center for Internet Security (CIS), offer valuable resources, alerts, and guidelines for staying secure.

2. Participate in Cybersecurity Training and Webinars

Continuing your education through cybersecurity training and webinars can deepen your understanding of security practices and help you stay ahead of new threats.

- **Online Courses**: Many platforms offer free or paid cybersecurity courses that cover various aspects of online security, from basic awareness to advanced defensive techniques. Websites like Coursera, Udemy, and Cybrary provide a range of courses suitable for all levels.

- **Webinars and Virtual Conferences**: Attend webinars and virtual conferences hosted by cybersecurity experts and organizations. These events often cover the latest developments in the field and provide practical advice for improving your security posture.

- **Workshops and Local Meetups**: If available, participate in local workshops or meetups focused on cybersecurity. These in-person events offer opportunities to learn from experts and network with others interested in cybersecurity.

3. Engage with Online Communities

Online communities and forums are valuable resources for sharing knowledge, asking questions, and learning from the experiences of others in the cybersecurity field.

- **Cybersecurity Forums**: Join cybersecurity forums such as Reddit's r/cybersecurity, Stack Exchange's Information Security community, or specialized forums like Bleeping Computer. These platforms allow you to discuss security topics, seek advice, and stay informed about the latest trends.

- **Social Media Groups**: Follow cybersecurity experts and groups on social media platforms like Twitter, LinkedIn, and Facebook. Engaging with these communities can help you stay current with industry news and connect with professionals who share your interests.

- **Email Newsletters**: Subscribe to email newsletters from trusted cybersecurity sources. Newsletters can provide curated content, insights, and tips directly to your inbox, making it easier to stay informed.

Creating a Personal Cybersecurity Plan

A personal cybersecurity plan brings together all the practices and strategies discussed in this handbook, providing you with a structured approach to ongoing protection. By creating and following a cybersecurity plan, you can ensure that your digital security remains strong and resilient over time.

1. Assess Your Risk Profile

Understanding your personal risk profile is the first step in creating an effective cybersecurity plan. This involves evaluating the types of data you handle, the devices you use, and the potential threats you face.

- **Identify Sensitive Data**: Determine what sensitive data you possess, such as financial information, personal identification details, or confidential business documents. Consider the potential impact if this data were to be compromised.

- **Evaluate Your Devices**: Take stock of the devices you use, including computers, smartphones, tablets, and IoT devices. Each device represents a potential entry point for cyber threats, and your plan should address the security needs of each.

- **Consider Potential Threats**: Think about the types of cyber threats you are most likely to encounter, based on your online activities, profession, and personal circumstances. For example, individuals working in finance or technology may be more targeted by phishing attacks or hacking attempts.

2. Set Security Goals

Based on your risk profile, establish clear security goals that you aim to achieve with your cybersecurity plan. These goals should be specific, measurable, and aligned with your needs.

- **Enhance Password Security**: One goal could be to improve password security across all your accounts by implementing a password manager and enabling two-factor authentication.

- **Secure All Devices**: Another goal might be to secure all your devices by ensuring that they are updated, encrypted, and protected by antivirus software.

- **Educate Yourself on Cybersecurity**: You might also set a goal to complete a certain number of cybersecurity courses or to stay regularly informed by reading cybersecurity news.

3. Implement Regular Security Practices

Incorporate regular security practices into your routine to maintain and strengthen your digital defenses over time.

- **Schedule Regular Security Checks**: Set aside time each month to review and update your passwords, check for software updates, and monitor account activity. Make this a non-negotiable part of your routine to ensure that your security remains up-to-date.

- **Perform Regular Backups**: Establish a regular backup schedule that works for you, whether it's daily, weekly, or monthly. Ensure that your backups are stored securely and verify their integrity periodically.

- **Stay Informed and Educated**: Commit to staying informed about cybersecurity trends by regularly reading news articles, attending webinars, or participating in online communities. Consider setting aside time each week to focus on cybersecurity education.

4. Review and Adapt Your Plan

Cybersecurity is an evolving field, and your personal cybersecurity plan should be flexible enough to adapt to new threats and changes in your life.

- **Regularly Review Your Plan**: Review your cybersecurity plan at least once a year to ensure it remains relevant and effective. Update it as necessary to reflect changes in your risk profile, new devices, or advancements in security technology.

- **Adapt to New Threats**: Stay vigilant for emerging threats and be prepared to adjust your plan accordingly. This might involve adopting new security practices, upgrading your software, or implementing additional security measures.

- Seek Professional Advice if Needed:
If you encounter challenges or feel
overwhelmed by the complexity of
cybersecurity, don't hesitate to seek
professional advice. Cybersecurity
professionals can provide tailored
recommendations, assist with implementing
advanced security measures, and help you
refine your personal cybersecurity plan.

5. Stay Flexible and Proactive
Your cybersecurity plan should not be static;
it should evolve as you gain more knowledge
and as the digital landscape changes.
Staying flexible and proactive in your
approach will enable you to respond
effectively to new challenges and maintain
strong defenses.

- Respond to Changes in Your Life:
Major life events, such as a new job, a move
to a new location, or the acquisition of new
devices, may require adjustments to your

cybersecurity plan. Be mindful of these changes and adapt your plan to address any new risks.

- **Monitor Emerging Technologies**: As technology advances, new tools and practices may become available to enhance your security. Stay informed about these developments and be open to integrating them into your routine.

- **Continuously Improve Your Skills**: Cybersecurity is an ongoing learning process. Continuously seek out opportunities to improve your skills and knowledge, whether through formal training, self-study, or engagement with the cybersecurity community.

Conclusion

As we conclude this cybersecurity handbook, it's essential to revisit the key lessons learned and the steps you can take to continue strengthening your cybersecurity practices. Cybersecurity is a dynamic and ever-evolving field, and while this handbook has provided you with foundational knowledge, your journey toward becoming more secure in the digital world is ongoing.

Recap of Key Points

Throughout this handbook, we've explored a wide range of topics that are crucial for protecting yourself and your digital assets. Let's summarize the key points:

1. Understanding the Basics

- **Cybersecurity Defined**: We began by defining cybersecurity as the practice of protecting systems, networks, and data from digital attacks. Understanding this concept is the first step in recognizing the importance of securing your online presence.

- **Key Terminologies**: We covered essential cybersecurity terms, such as firewalls, encryption, and malware. Familiarity with these terms is critical for navigating the cybersecurity landscape and making informed decisions.

- **How Cyber Attacks Happen**: You learned about the basic methods used by hackers to breach systems, including phishing, malware, and social engineering. Awareness of these tactics can help you identify potential threats before they cause harm.

2. **Securing Your Devices**
- **Personal Computers**: We discussed the importance of basic security measures for

your personal computers, such as keeping your software updated, using antivirus programs, and enabling firewalls. These steps form the foundation of your digital security.

- **Mobile Devices**: Securing your mobile devices is equally important, and we covered best practices such as using strong passwords, enabling two-factor authentication, and being cautious about app permissions.

- **IoT Devices**: With the rise of smart devices, securing your Internet of Things (IoT) gadgets has become crucial. We emphasized the importance of updating firmware, changing default passwords, and securing your home network.

3. Safe Internet Practices
- **Recognizing Phishing Scams**: We provided tips on how to identify and avoid phishing scams, which remain one of the most common and effective methods used

by cybercriminals to steal personal information.

- **Creating Strong Passwords**: The creation and management of strong passwords are vital to keeping your accounts secure. We discussed the characteristics of strong passwords and the use of password managers to help manage them effectively.

- **Using Public Wi-Fi Safely**: Public Wi-Fi networks can be a significant security risk. We highlighted the dangers and provided strategies for staying safe, such as using VPNs and avoiding sensitive transactions on public networks.

4. Protecting Your Online Identity

- **Social Media Security**: Social media platforms are prime targets for cyber threats. We explored how to secure your social media accounts, manage privacy settings, and be cautious about the information you share online.

- **Email Security**: Emails are another common attack vector. We covered best practices for email security, including avoiding spam, recognizing phishing emails, and using encrypted email services.

- **Managing Personal Information**: Managing the sharing of your personal information online is critical for protecting your identity. We discussed strategies for limiting the exposure of sensitive data and using privacy tools to enhance security.

5. Data Protection and Privacy

- **Importance of Backups**: Regular backups are your safety net in case of data loss due to cyber attacks, hardware failures, or accidental deletions. We reviewed the different methods available for backing up your data securely.

- **Understanding Encryption**: Encryption is a powerful tool for protecting your data. We explained the basics of encryption and how to use encryption tools to safeguard your sensitive information.

- Privacy Tools: We provided an overview of tools like VPNs, secure browsers, and privacy-focused apps that can help you maintain your privacy online and protect your data from prying eyes.

6. Responding to Cyber Threats

- **What to Do in Case of a Breach**: We outlined the steps to take if your accounts or devices are compromised, emphasizing the importance of acting quickly to mitigate damage.
- **Reporting Cybercrime**: Knowing how and when to report cybercrime is crucial. We discussed the appropriate channels for reporting incidents and the importance of documenting evidence.
- **Recovering from Cyber Attacks**: Recovery from a cyber attack requires a systematic approach. We provided tips on minimizing damage, restoring systems, and learning from the experience to prevent future incidents.

7. Building a Cybersecurity Routine

- **Regular Security Checks**: Establishing a routine of regular security checks is essential for maintaining strong digital defenses. We emphasized the importance of updating passwords, monitoring account activity, and performing regular backups.

- **Staying Informed**: The cybersecurity landscape is constantly changing, and staying informed about the latest threats and trends is crucial. We discussed resources for ongoing education and the importance of continuous learning.

- **Creating a Personal Cybersecurity Plan**: Finally, we encouraged you to create a personal cybersecurity plan that brings together all the practices discussed in this handbook. This plan will serve as your roadmap to ongoing protection.

Taking the Next Steps

The knowledge and skills you've gained from this handbook are a powerful foundation, but cybersecurity is a field that requires ongoing attention and effort. As you continue your journey, here are some next steps to consider:

1. Continue Learning

Cybersecurity is an ever-evolving field, with new threats and technologies emerging regularly. To stay ahead of potential risks, commit to continuous learning.

- **Enroll in Cybersecurity Courses**: Consider taking additional courses that delve deeper into specific areas of cybersecurity, such as network security, ethical hacking, or data protection. Many online platforms offer courses for all skill levels.

- **Attend Webinars and Conferences**: Participate in cybersecurity webinars and conferences to stay informed about the latest trends and best practices. These events often feature insights from industry experts and opportunities for networking.

- **Join Cybersecurity Communities**: Engage with online communities and forums where you can share knowledge, ask questions, and learn from the experiences of others. Communities like Reddit's r/cybersecurity or the Information Security Stack Exchange are excellent places to start.

2. Apply What You've Learned

Knowledge is most valuable when it's put into practice. Take the information you've gained from this handbook and apply it to your daily digital life.

- **Implement a Cybersecurity Routine**: If you haven't already, start building your cybersecurity routine. Schedule regular security checks, keep your software updated, and make a habit of staying informed about the latest threats.

- **Develop a Personal Cybersecurity Plan**: Use the framework provided in Chapter 7 to create a personal cybersecurity plan tailored to your specific needs and risk profile. This plan will help guide your ongoing efforts to stay secure.

- Educate Others: Share what you've learned with friends, family, or colleagues. Helping others improve their cybersecurity practices not only benefits them but also contributes to a safer online community overall.

3. Stay Vigilant

Cyber threats are constantly evolving, and staying vigilant is key to maintaining your security.

- **Monitor for New Threats**: Regularly check trusted cybersecurity sources for news about emerging threats and vulnerabilities. Staying informed will help you adapt your security practices as needed.

- Review and Adapt Your Security Plan: Periodically review your cybersecurity plan to ensure it remains effective. Be prepared to adapt it in response to changes in your life, new technologies, or emerging threats.

- Don't Become Complacent: Cybersecurity is not a one-time task but an ongoing responsibility. Avoid becoming complacent by maintaining your routine and staying proactive about your security.

Final Thoughts

The digital world offers incredible opportunities, but it also comes with risks that must be managed. By taking cybersecurity seriously and applying the knowledge you've gained from this handbook, you can protect yourself, your data, and your online identity from the myriad threats that exist today.

Remember, cybersecurity is not just about the tools and technologies you use—it's about cultivating a mindset of awareness, caution, and continuous improvement. As you move forward, stay committed to learning, adapting, and strengthening your cybersecurity practices.

Your efforts in building and maintaining strong cybersecurity habits will pay off in the long run, giving you the confidence and peace of mind to navigate the digital landscape safely. The journey doesn't end here—continue to educate yourself, stay vigilant, and protect your digital life with the same care and attention you would give to any other valuable aspect of your life.

By taking these steps, you are not only securing your own digital presence but also contributing to the broader effort to create a safer and more secure online world for everyone.

Appendices

The appendices serve as a valuable resource to reinforce and complement the information provided throughout the handbook. They offer quick references, practical tools, and actionable steps that can help you put your newfound cybersecurity knowledge into practice.

Glossary of Cybersecurity Terms

Cybersecurity can be a jargon-heavy field, and understanding the key terms is crucial for making informed decisions. This glossary provides definitions of essential cybersecurity terms mentioned in the handbook.

- **Antivirus**: Software designed to detect and remove malicious software (malware) from computers and devices. It scans files and programs to identify and eliminate threats.

- **Authentication**: The process of verifying the identity of a user or device, typically through passwords, biometric data, or security tokens, to grant access to systems or information.

- **Backup**: The practice of creating copies of data to protect against loss or corruption. Backups can be stored locally (on an external hard drive) or remotely (in the cloud).

- **Botnet**: A network of compromised computers controlled by a hacker, often used to conduct large-scale attacks, such as distributed denial-of-service (DDoS) attacks.

- **Cryptography**: The practice of securing information by converting it into a code to prevent unauthorized access. Encryption is a form of cryptography.

- **DDoS Attack**: A type of cyber attack where multiple systems flood the bandwidth or resources of a targeted system, usually one or more web servers, causing them to become overwhelmed and unavailable.

- **Encryption**: The process of converting data into a secure format that is unreadable without a decryption key. This protects information from unauthorized access.

- **Firewall**: A security device or software that monitors and controls incoming and outgoing network traffic based on predetermined security rules, acting as a barrier between a trusted network and untrusted networks.

- **Malware**: Malicious software designed to harm, exploit, or otherwise compromise a computer system. Common types include viruses, worms, and ransomware.

- **Multi-Factor Authentication (MFA)**: A security process that requires two or more forms of verification before granting access to a system or account. MFA enhances security by adding an extra layer of protection beyond just a password.

- **Phishing**: A social engineering attack where a cybercriminal poses as a legitimate entity to trick individuals into revealing sensitive information, such as passwords or credit card numbers.

- **Ransomware**: A type of malware that encrypts a victim's data and demands a ransom payment in exchange for the decryption key.

- **Social Engineering**: A tactic used by cybercriminals to manipulate individuals into divulging confidential information.

Techniques often involve psychological manipulation, such as pretending to be a trusted person or authority.

- **Spyware**: Malicious software that secretly monitors and collects information about a user's activities, often without their knowledge. This information can be used for identity theft or other malicious purposes.

- **Two-Factor Authentication (2FA)**: A method of confirming a user's identity by requiring two separate types of authentication factors, typically something the user knows (password) and something they have (a smartphone or security token).

- **Virtual Private Network (VPN)**: A service that encrypts your internet connection and routes it through a server in a different location, providing anonymity and security by masking your IP address and online activities.

- **Vulnerability**: A weakness in a computer system, network, or software that can be exploited by cybercriminals to gain unauthorized access or cause harm.

- **Worm**: A type of malware that replicates itself and spreads across networks, often without any human intervention, causing widespread damage.

Useful Tools and Resources

Equipping yourself with the right tools and resources is essential for maintaining strong cybersecurity practices. Here's a list of software, websites, and organizations that can help you enhance your digital security.

1. **Security Software**
- **Antivirus Programs**:
    - **Norton Antivirus**: Offers comprehensive protection against malware,

viruses, and other threats with real-time scanning and automatic updates.

- **McAfee Total Protection**: Provides multi-device security, including antivirus, firewall, and identity theft protection.

- **Bitdefender Antivirus Plus**: Known for its high detection rates and low system impact, Bitdefender offers advanced threat defense and multi-layer ransomware protection.

- **Password Managers:**

- **LastPass**: A popular password manager that stores and encrypts your passwords, making it easy to manage strong, unique passwords for every account.

- **1Password**: Offers secure password storage, password generation, and features like Travel Mode to protect sensitive information while traveling.

- **Dashlane**: Provides password management, secure storage for sensitive information, and dark web monitoring for compromised accounts.

- **VPN Services**:

   - **ExpressVPN**: Offers fast and secure VPN services with a wide range of server locations, strong encryption, and a strict no-logs policy.

   - **NordVPN**: Provides double encryption, a large network of servers, and additional security features like CyberSec to block ads and malware.

   - **CyberGhost**: A user-friendly VPN service with strong privacy features, including a no-logs policy and automatic kill switch.

- **Encryption Tools**:

   - **VeraCrypt**: An open-source encryption tool that allows you to create encrypted volumes or encrypt entire drives.

   - **BitLocker (Windows)**: A built-in encryption tool for Windows that allows you to encrypt entire drives, including the system drive.

- **GnuPG (GNU Privacy Guard)**: An open-source encryption tool that allows you to encrypt files, emails, and directories with strong cryptography.

2. Educational Resources
- Websites and Blogs:
- **Krebs on Security**: A leading blog by cybersecurity expert Brian Krebs, providing in-depth analysis of security news and threats.
- **Cybrary**: An online learning platform offering free and paid cybersecurity courses, certifications, and resources.
- **The Hacker News**: A popular cybersecurity news website covering the latest threats, vulnerabilities, and trends.

- Organizations:
- **The National Cyber Security Alliance (NCSA)**: A nonprofit organization that provides cybersecurity awareness and education through initiatives like Cybersecurity Awareness Month.

- **The Electronic Frontier Foundation (EFF)**: An organization dedicated to defending civil liberties in the digital world, offering guides on privacy and security.

- **SANS Institute**: A leading provider of cybersecurity training and certification, offering resources for both beginners and professionals.

3. Online Tools and Scanners

- **VirusTotal**: A free online service that analyzes files and URLs for viruses, worms, trojans, and other malware.

- **Have I Been Pwned?**: A website that allows you to check if your email address has been compromised in a data breach.

- **Shodan**: A search engine that scans the internet for connected devices, allowing you to identify vulnerabilities in your networked devices.

Sample Cybersecurity Checklist

To help you start securing your digital life, this sample checklist provides actionable steps that you can follow. This checklist can serve as a guide for building your cybersecurity routine.

1. **Secure Your Devices**
- **Update Operating Systems**: Ensure that your computer, smartphone, and other devices are running the latest operating systems with all security patches applied.
- **Install Antivirus Software**: Use reputable antivirus software and keep it updated to protect against malware.
- **Enable Firewalls**: Turn on firewalls on all devices to monitor and control incoming and outgoing network traffic.
- **Secure IoT Devices**: Change default passwords, update firmware, and consider placing IoT devices on a separate network.

2. **Protect Your Accounts**

- **Create Strong Passwords**: Use complex, unique passwords for each account. Consider using a password manager to manage them.

- **Enable Two-Factor Authentication (2FA)**: Wherever possible, enable 2FA to add an extra layer of security to your accounts.

- **Review Account Settings**: Regularly review the privacy and security settings of your online accounts, especially on social media platforms.

- **Monitor Account Activity**: Keep an eye on your account activity and enable alerts for suspicious logins or transactions.

3. Practice Safe Internet Habits

- **Recognize Phishing Attempts**: Be cautious of unsolicited emails and messages asking for sensitive information. Verify the sender before clicking on links or downloading attachments.

- **Use a VPN**: When using public Wi-Fi, use a VPN to encrypt your internet connection and protect your data.
- Avoid Sharing Personal Information: Limit the amount of personal information you share online, especially on social media.

4. Protect Your Data

- **Back Up Regularly**: Set up automatic backups for your important files and data. Use both local and cloud-based backup solutions.
- **Encrypt Sensitive Data**: Use encryption tools to protect sensitive files and communications from unauthorized access.
- **Secure Physical Devices**: Lock your devices with strong passwords or biometric authentication, and keep them in secure locations when not in use.

Response to Cyber Threats

1. Signs of a Breach:

- **Unusual Activity**: Monitor for any unusual behavior on your accounts, such as login attempts from unknown locations, unauthorized transactions, or unexpected password changes.

- **Unexpected Software**: Watch out for unfamiliar apps or programs that appear on your devices without your knowledge, as they could indicate malware or spyware.

- **Strange Messages**: Be cautious if you receive odd messages or emails from your contacts, which could indicate that their accounts have been compromised and are being used for phishing attacks.

2. **Immediate Response**:

- **Disconnect from Networks**: If you suspect a breach, disconnect the affected device from the internet and any connected networks to prevent further spread of malware or data theft.

- **Change Passwords**: Immediately change the passwords for any compromised accounts. If possible, do this from a different, secure device.

- **Scan for Malware**: Run a full scan with your antivirus software to detect and remove any malicious programs or files.

3. **Report the Incident**:

- **Contact Authorities**: Report the cyber attack to local law enforcement or a national cybercrime reporting center, such as the FBI's Internet Crime Complaint Center (IC3) in the U.S.

- **Notify Affected Parties**: Inform any individuals or organizations that may have been impacted by the breach, especially if their personal information was exposed.

4. **Recover and Strengthen Security:**

- **Restore from Backup**: If necessary, restore your data from a secure backup. Ensure that your backup is clean and free from any malware.

- **Review Security Measures**: Evaluate and strengthen your cybersecurity practices, such as updating security software, enabling two-factor authentication, and reviewing account settings.

 - **Seek Professional Help**: Consider consulting a cybersecurity professional if the breach is severe or if you need help securing your systems and data.

This appendix is designed to serve as a practical guide for readers to implement the cybersecurity knowledge they've gained from the handbook. By following the glossary, using recommended tools, and adhering to the checklist, readers can establish a robust defense against the ever-evolving landscape of cyber threats. The tools and resources provided empower users to take control of their digital security, while the sample checklist offers a straightforward, actionable plan for protecting themselves online.